FLAVOR FLAV

the icon the memoir

Farrah Gray Publishing

www.fgpbooks.com

ISBN-13: 978-0-9827-0277-2
ISBN-10: 0-9827-0277-9
ISBN-13: 978-0-9727-0992-7 (e-books)
ISBN-10: 0-9727-0992-4 (e-books)

Publisher: Farrah Gray Publishing
        P.O. Box 33355
        Las Vegas, NV 89133

Art Director: Andre Akil
Karyn Langhorne Folan
Dr. Marcia Brevard Wynn
Cover Photo ©Flavor Flav

In Loving Memory of

Elizabeth Drayton (my great-grandmother),

Estella Maude Smith (my father's mother),

Mary Bailey Deleston (my mother's mother),

William Drayton, Sr. (my father),

Joey Bartone (my dear friend)

and

Jack Hamilton (my dear friend)

Table of Contents

PART TWO
The Breaking of Flavor Flav

PART THREE
Recreating Flavor Flav

Introduction

OKAY, FOLKS. Let me take you on a little journey...

I'm hanging from the bottom step of a ladder, deep in the well of a manhole on the 59th Street Bridge connecting Queens to Manhattan. When I look down between my dangling feet, there's a 180 foot drop into the East River. There ain't nothing between me and the water but space. Nothing but air, man. I'm just hanging there, straining my muscles, fingers gripping the metal, listening to the rush of the air around me, the sounds of the water below me, the rumble of traffic over my head.

Scared?

Nah. Not at all. I've been a daredevil with my life—all my life. By the time I decided to scramble down that manhole and see what was there, I'd already busted my head wide open falling off of a car ramp when I was five years old, and

broken my leg and my arm falling from a four-story building
—and those are just the ones I can remember right now. I'd
always wanted to walk across a bridge—don't ask me why,
I just wanted to—so I hopped off the bus that I was riding
into the city and started walking. When I saw the manhole,
it didn't have a cover or nothing and it was like "Wowwww!"
I dared myself to do it and I did it. I climbed in that manhole.
When I realized there wasn't anything down there but the
East River and that long drop into it, I kept going.

Why? 'Cause it was there, man. Do I need a better reason?

Okay, so here's a better reason—I like excitement. I *need*
it. I'm an adrenaline junkie and I always have been. More
than anything else, the need for excitement drives me. It
keeps me bouncing from one project to the next, keeps me
moving, and keeps me seeking the next thrill. Excitement,
man. It was my first addiction and is the one that I'll never,
ever kick. I was happy as hell swinging on the last step of
that ladder, with nobody to bother me, staring down at the
river, knowing that if I slipped just a little, it would be over.
Bye Flav. Time's up, boy!

But God is good. I didn't slip. I was getting kinda tired,
though, after hanging there for a long time, so I took my
right hand and reached up a step. Then I did the same with
my left, until little by little I got my legs back up on the ladder and I climbed back up to the street. I bet the people driving in their cars over that bridge thought it was crazy as hell

when they saw a skinny black man pop up out of the man-hole like it wasn't shit and start walking across the bridge!

Twenty years later, I walked across that same bridge again, looking for the same manhole. It was gone. The city must have closed it up, and sealed it off. That first time, I was meant to find it, but the second time, man, I guess it wasn't meant for me to find.

I guess that might have been because, in those twenty years since I climbed down that manhole, my life had been a thrill ride. A real roller coaster, folks. I was climbing to the highest heights, then rushing down into some pretty deep holes, then climbing again back up to the heights. In those twenty years, I had been called everything from "the great-est hype man ever" to "a crackhead." People knew me for my music and my years with *Public Enemy*, one of the most influ-ential hip-hop groups ever. Then they knew me because of my struggles with addiction and the law. Just like a roller coaster, that wasn't the end of your boy. I came back up again with a whole new career on television with a string of hit reality shows.

I'm telling this story because in a lot of ways, climbing into and out of that manhole is the story of my whole life. Searching for excitement has gotten me all kinds of fantas-tic opportunities, and it still does. It's also gotten me into plenty of trouble. I cannot tell a lie. No matter how much trouble I got into, I somehow always found a way to get myself out of it. I've climbed into many holes in my life, but I've also found the strength to climb back out.

I'd do it all again. All of it—or most of it, anyway. No regrets, folks. Your boy doesn't play that game. Along the way, I've met people who love me, and I've clashed with people who don't. Love me or hate me, the one word that people keep using to describe me is "icon."

Icon.

Yeah, boy. I like it. I like it a *lot*.

This is the story behind the image, folks. This is the story of the real man and his real struggles, naw'mean? I'm telling it straight, laying it down for you *for real* because that's the only way I know how to do it. It's gonna get gritty, 'cause I've been down some pretty dark holes, but for all the depths, there are heights, too. No matter how far down I've been, I've never stopped climbing. If there's one message I'd send to you, the reader of these pages, it's that it doesn't matter how deep the hole gets, *you* gotta keep climbing, too.

And that's the truth, man, naw'mean?

Kirk, out!!

PART ONE

The Making of "Flavor Flav"

Chapter One

It's All in the Name:
The Birth of "Flavor Flav"

I T ALL STARTED WITH A JOINT of angel dust and a couple of garbage bags full of black spray paint.

Well, it really started 17 years before that, on March 16, 1959, the day I was born. But on that day, folks, my mom, Anna E. Drayton, didn't look at her baby boy and say, "I think I'll name him Flavor Flav!"

Nah, you know *that* never happened!

You probably saw my moms on *Flavor of Love*, and if you did, you know she's a very good, very religious, straight-up type of woman. She named me "William Jonathan Drayton, Jr.," and in my family they called me "Ricco" as a nickname. I don't know why. It was something my uncle, Charles Higgs, came up with.

This book is about Flavor Flav, and if you want to know when *he* was born, it goes back to that joint of angel dust. By angel dust, I mean PCP, y'all.

I gave myself the name "Flavor" and then Chuck D stretched it out to "Flavor Flav" a few years later. He didn't know what he was starting!

Hee, hee, har, har—that's me laughing, folks. Every time you see those words, you can think to yourself, "Flav's cracking up!"

Seriously, not even I would have guessed that people all over the world would know me as "Flavor Flav" and that I would answer to it like it was the name I was born with. I just wanted a name that would set me apart from all the other wannabe DJs and MCs in New York.

This was in the late 1970s and early 80s, naw'mean? Hip hop music was just beginning to separate itself from soul, disco and funk. People had been DJ-ing for a while, but the idea of talking over the record and hyping the crowd as the master of ceremonies, the "MC," was pretty new.

Also, to let y'all know, I was one of the first original DJs on Long Island. There wasn't no such thing as a mixer. DJs had a turntable and radio and as the record was going off on the turntable, we would be turning up the song that was playing on the radio. When the song on the radio was going off, we started mixing in the record that was on the turntable. That's what we called DJ-ing, folks. Then we started blending and mixing the two so you had continuous music and little blending. Then the mixer was created and people started using "echo chambers." Everyone was doing their parties with the echos. Next thing you know, people started rhyming, and it was just very organic. The first rap record I ever heard was Fatback Band's "King Tim III" in 1980.

That's the record that started everybody emceeing and rapping.

Yeah, your boy wanted to be a real MC and all the MC's had common names, like MC Philly Phil, MC Bobby Bob, and MC Mikey D. Now you *know* that wasn't for me. I didn't see myself as MC Willy Will or Billy Bill or any shit like that. So I said to myself, "You need a name that nobody else has. That nobody else would want. But the name has to mean something." It couldn't just be some stupid name for the sake of a name.

I didn't want to use "Ricco." I didn't feel like it had the right sound for an MC, naw'mean? Listen to it—"DJ Ricco Ric." Nothin' there man. Nothin' for folks to latch on to or remember. I was thinkin' and thinkin' about what my name could be. Then I remembered the nickname that had been floating around me for a few years—"Flavor Freak."

"Flavor Freak" was a nickname given to me by this guy named Kevin Starks, who had known me since I was a baby. His grandmother, Mimi Starks, who everyone called "Miz Mimi," used to babysit me. Kevin started calling me "Ric the

Flavor Freak." (The way we pronounce "Ricco" in my family, see, the "ric" rhymes with "freak.")

Why did he call me "Ric the Flavor Freak?"

Hell, I don't know! Kevin was probably high when he thought of it—he was high a lot. Hee, hee, har, har!

Seriously, folks, it started because I was always drinking flavored sodas, and sucking on Lifesavers and stuff like that. I liked those bright sweet tastes—red, yellow, orange, and green. Kevin said I was "A freak for flavor" and started calling me "Flavor Freak."

No one else called me that and it had never really stuck, but I kinda liked it because it was kinda true.

Flavor Freak wasn't much of an MC name, but "MC Flavor?" I thought that might work. Since I was a DJ trying to become an MC, I decided the better name was "MC/DJ Flavor."

I had a MC/DJ name, but I didn't have a reputation.

So, there I was, sitting around my mother's house in Roosevelt, Long Island with my cousin Stewie—Stewart Addison, is his name. I was getting dusted and thinking about how I was gonna be this big MC/DJ. I guess I got so dusted that I started to trip off that. I went down to the basement, got two garbage bags full of black spray paint, and Stewie and I hit the street.

What?

You wanna know what I was doing with two garbage bags full of black spray paint in my basement?

Good question.

Let's just say I had a stash of spray paint, 15 full bags of the stuff, sitting down there in my mom's basement, waiting for their moment. Back in the day, your boy wasn't exactly a choir boy. As a teenager, I did my share of boosting and vandalism. I'm not proud of it, and I don't steal from anyone now that I'm clean and drug-free, but back then, it was a different story.

So, on this particular day, as I said, there just happened to be a lot of spray paint in the basement, okay? I was dusted out of my mind, got an idea, went down in the basement and got two bags of spray paint from my stash.

Stewie carried one bag and I carried the other one. We walked from my mother's house all the way to the projects on Albany Avenue and Buffalo Avenue in Freeport, Long Island, maybe 3 miles or so. On every single corner, I sprayed my new tag:

"FLAVOR."

That's right, folks. I wrote my name on every sidewalk, on every wall, and on every corner from Roosevelt to the projects in Freeport. I even tagged the Freeport train station of the Long Island Railroad. I tagged the side of the Goodyear Tire place. If there was a building on the corner, I sprayed "Flavor" on it.

I was dusted and I just didn't give a fuck!

When I think about it now, it's like wooowwwww...

The next morning everybody woke up and it was all over the place. "Who's this Flavor?" "Who's the Flavor who wrote his name all over everything from Roosevelt all the way to the projects in Freeport?"

No one knew who Flavor was.

And me? I was just sitting back laughing, and waiting.

Finally my cousin, Makeva Higgs, figured it out. She asked me, "Are you Flavor?"

"Yeah," I said, and I told her it was my new MC/DJ name.

She was like, "Eww, Ricco, that's ugly. That's an ugly name. Why you wanna call yourself that?"

I said, "Because it's different and nobody likes it and that's why I'm gonna stick with it."

And my cousin, Makeva? She's proud of me now. Me and my ugly ass name.

The story of how my name went from "DJ Flavor" to Flavor Flav is also the story of how I got hooked up with my partner Chuck D and the Shockley brothers, Hank and Keith. It's partly my story, and partly the story of *Public Enemy*.

Chapter Two

Flavor and Public Enemy

I WAS WALKING THROUGH the graveyard—at night. Musta have been late 1984. I remember it was winter because it was cold as hell and already pitch dark at 7 p.m.

I was following this path between the headstones. It was really dark and your boy was kinda creeped out, naw'mean, even though I'd walked that path a hundred times. Something about walking in a graveyard at night gets your boy's mind goin' in strange directions. I remember walking through that graveyard, thinking about *"Dark Shadows,"* a TV show that was one of my favorites coming up, and *Night of the Living Dead* and shit like that.

I was walking fast, not just because I was thinking about

all that horror movie shit, but because I had to get to the studio. I had something very exciting to tell my partner, Chuck D.

I rushed through the gravestones, man, then walked down a long street to the studio at 510 South Franklin Avenue in Hempstead, Long Island and climbed the stairs. Almost as soon as I got to the studio door, I heard music—a real long tone, with a fucking slamming beat beneath it. Slamming, Gee. That music was *slamming*! The song that Chuck was using was called "Blow Your Head." I walked in the studio and Chuck had a cassette tape coming out of the machine, going around the mike stand and back into the machine. I'd never seen anyone do that before.

"What the fuck is you doing?" I asked him.

Little do y'all know, folks, Chuck D had created the first loop in the history of music. Incredible!!! The music was the track that eventually became the song "Public Enemy Number One," and the loop completely changed the sound of music, man. It was just sick, how good that shit sounded.

Then I told him about what happened to me at the bus stop.

If you've heard "Public Enemy Number One," you already *know* what happened at the bus stop.

I said:

*Yo, Chuck, bust a move, man. I was on my way up here to
the studio, you know what I'm sayin', and this brother stopped
me and asked me, "Yo wassup with yo boy Chucky D? He
swear he nice." I said," Yo, the brother don't swear he nice, he
knows he nice, you know what I'm sayin?" So, Chuck, I got a
feeling you turning into a public enemy, man. Now, remember
that line you was kickin' to me on the way out to LA Laurelton
Queens while we was in the car on the way to the shop? Well,
yo, right now kick that bass for them brothers and let them
know what goes on...*

The whole story is longer, but when Chuck D said, "Yo,
Ricco, take that story and put it on the beginning of this
tape," that was what we came up with.

That was the beginning of *Public Enemy's* first single ever,
"Public Enemy #1."

Now, this is something a lot of people don't know about
me. Yeah, I'm a hype man, the greatest hype man ever in
the game, naw'mean, but whatever else I might have been
or done, I've always been known for music, man. I started
playing the piano at the age of five, mostly teaching myself.
I started singing in church around that age, too. Shortly
after that, I picked up the drums, the bass guitar, then the
trombone, the tuba, the clarinet, the French horn, the vio-
lin, the trumpet, the saxophone, then the xylophone. Then
I started playing kettle drums and I climbed up on a chair

and learned how to play the oboe. I can also play a cello and African drums (which we call congas), bongos, timbales, cow bells and synthesizers.

In high school, I used to cut my classes and spend the day sitting in the band room, trying out one instrument after the other. Right now, I play over 15 different instruments, but I can't read a lick of music, folks. Not one note. But if I hear it, I got it. Get it?

Hee, hee, har, har!

All through high school, which wasn't very long, though, because I dropped out in the 10th grade, I had bands. My band won the variety show at Freeport High School in 1978! The group was called *Sweet Funk* and we played an original song that I wrote, called "The Brass Monster."

I tell you this because, if it weren't for the fact that I was musical, and that I can play just about anything, I never would been standin' in that studio, telling Chuck D about what happened to me at the bus stop.

Time for a flashback, folks.

Okay, so now it's like 1982 or 1983. Don't expect me to be precise, man. First, it was a long time ago now, almost 30 years! Second, I've done a lot of drugs in my life. A looooot of drugs. So I'm writing this book to tell you about a lot of the mistakes with drugs in my life and I how I corrected them. And it's no lie. So 'scuse me if I don't got the dates completely right in my head.

Anyway, it's like 1982 or 1983, and my boy TA, Tony Allen, was part of a rap group called *Townhouse Three* that was made up of TA, a guy named Pep, and a guy named Jowell (Jeffery Howell). TA and I were best friends. He and his group were working with a guy called "Chucky D" and his partner, Hank Boxley, making a tape for WBAU, the radio station out at Adelphi University in Garden City, New York. WBAU used to play local musicians' music on certain shows, and these guys were putting something together for that.

So, TA was like, "Hey man, I need you to come out to the studio with me and play this riff on the keyboard for us."

TA was my boy, so I went. That was really the first time I met Chuck (whose real name is Carlton Ridenhour), and Hank and Keith Boxley. I knew them from their reps as DJs, but we had never hung out until that night. I played one of those little electric keyboards for them, and they recorded the riff for their tape. When we finished with the music part, we were just sitting at the studio, hanging out.

We started playing the dozens, man.

Now if there's one thing you need to know about your boy, Flavor Flav, it's that I love to play the dozens, and I'm good at it, too. No one beats me, man. *No one.*

So we're playing the dozens and, of course, I was the best. Like I said, no one beats me at the dozens. No one could out snap your boy, Ricco Drayton, MC/DJ Flavor. I'm telling the truth. I was so good, they all teamed up on me, and all by myself, I was taking them down.

These were deep, ugly, dirty, nasty snaps, naw'mean?

I told Hank, "Your grandmother's so broke, she driving your grandpa's casket on wheels around town."

I told Chuck his mother was so hungry she was digging up dead people for soup bones.

Serious, serious snaps, but we were laughing and having a good time, too. There was no way those guys were gonna forget Ricco Drayton, MC/DJ Flavor, soon to become Flavor Flav!

Some time went by, maybe a couple of weeks. I decided to go back to the studio and see what was going on with Chuck and Hank and those guys. That time, TA wasn't with me, and Chuck, Keith, and Hank and I were just snapping and hanging out. They had a mobile DJ group called *Spectrum* that used to go around to all the neighborhood parks, set up, and have "park jams"—playing Roosevelt Park, Camel Park in Hempstead, Hempstead Lake State Park, MLK Center and Rockville Center, and places like that. A lot of groups came out of *Spectrum* and got their start performing in those park jams, like *Leaders of the New School*. We were the ones who gave Busta Rhymes his name.

I was hanging with Hank, Chuck and Keith more and more, and I ended up helping them out with *Spectrum*. At first it was just helping to carry equipment and setting up for the jams, a process that used to take hours and hours. Then I was on the mike a lot, emceeing and getting the party hyped up, and yeah boy, I was good at that, too naw'mean? Things ended up going so well with me and *Spectrum* that I became one of them.

That's how I got hooked up with Chuck D, and Hank and Keith Shockley—Shockley was their stage name. I knew Richard Griffin (Griff), long before I was involved with *Spectrum*, but he had a security company that Hank and Keith used for the park jams, so we started to be around each other more once I was a member of *Spectrum*. I was hyping and rocking the microphone for a few years with *Spectrum* before *Public Enemy* was created and became big, and Griff was involved, too, so we knew each other. I can't say that we ever really hung out like Chuck, Hank, Keith and I did.

By now it's like the 1983 or 84. Like I said, Chuck was a college boy and so was Hank. They had a friend named Bill Stephney, who had a show on Adelphi University's college radio station, and they were always putting together groups and sending over tapes for Bill to play on his show. I didn't go to Adelphi (like I said, I never finished high school, man), but somehow they got me a show on WBAU on Thursday nights from 10 p.m. to 11:30 p.m.

It was the *MC/DJ Flavor Show*, of course. After my show came the *Spectrum City Mix Hour and One Half*, which was Chuck, Hank and Keith's show.

My format?

Simple.

What I was doing was walking around the neighborhoods collecting tapes that people made. As long as there weren't any curse words in it (which would get me in a whole lot of trouble), I'd play those home-made tapes, along with all the current hits. People tuned in 'cause having their jam on the radio made them feel like stars. Everybody had a tape back then, just like now. Everyone was trying to break into hip-hop or launch their group, just like now, naw'mean?

Meanwhile, I had some of everybody in the business come through my show, back then. Everyone that was hot on records was coming by to talk to us at the radio station—people like *Run DMC, Fat Boys*, LL Cool J and a bunch of others. We gave the *Fatboys* their very first radio interview. To this day Prince Markie Dee will tell you that WBAU and my show and Chuck's show, *The Spectrum City Mix Hour*, were his first interviews.

I loved doing radio, man. I even took a course for my AM radio license, but I never went back and got the FM license because I got locked up for a few weeks, probably for possession of a little marijuana, which in New York is only a little bit of jail time. I missed the test. When I got out, I'd lost my focus. It's too bad in a way, because that show was doing so well that it was beating out the commercial radio shows. I might have had me a career as a radio jock, but I guess, in the end, I had something better—a career on the radio as an artist, man!

Yeah, your boy was up there spinning records at the college, without having to take any classes! I did take a few, though. Thanks to John Schmidt, who let me take communications courses up there at Adelphi without enrolling in the degree program. Thanks, Gee!

Man, was my show popular! It became so popular that I actually had a fan club, naw'mean?

My fan club was called "The Flavortronz." By the time the show finished, I had 1,587 members. I know because I made their membership cards myself. Typed and printed out each card with my own hands, naw'mean? Why go to all that trouble? Because when you have fans, when you have people behind you, you got power, man.

That's something I haven't ever forgotten, man. If you're smart, you'll be good to your fans. Without them, you ain't got nothing.

Other than having a few fans and being on the radio, being MC/DJ Flavor hadn't changed my life much at that point. I was still in and out of jail, mostly for drug possession, but since I never got caught with more than a few ounces on me, I never did more than a couple weeks of time. I was still working all kinds of odd jobs, like security at Beacon Theater in Manhattan, where I got to meet Grace Jones and Frankie "Hollywood" Crocker. I did some institutional cooking at the Nassau County Courthouse, and then for Uniondale High School's cafeteria. I drove a school bus until I was in a wreck and lost my license. Yeah, you might have read something about me and a driver's license, but that problem goes waaaay back. I'll tell you about that later. For now, lemme tell you, it was sort of hand-to-mouth for your boy. I was bouncing from job to job while running my radio show and working with Chuck D and his father, driving U-Haul trucks for interior designers and decorators. We were making deliveries in Yonkers, New York, all around Manhattan and all over Long Island.

Delivering furniture to rich people, that's what we were doing.

I was also emceeing with Spectrum.

I was also selling drugs, of course. Can't leave that out. That was my other little sideline business. Later, I'd become my own biggest customer, but not yet.

I'd met this fine girl named Karren Ross one day at the radio station. She came up to the station with her brother Flashmaster D—Darren Ross. She had on this lime green dress, and you know I'm sucker for those bright colors and flavors. I had to have her.

We fell in love, man. She was the first girl I was that serious about. Serious enough to move in with. I had her leave her mom's house and move in with me and my mom. I needed to take care of my girl, so I did all those jobs. Every now and then, I'd make some serious money, but not like when I worked security for the Holmes-Ali fight. I charged people $250 a head to sneak in the back door of the Beacon Theater. I think I let about 130 people in for that one, man.

That was some serious cash. You do the math.

That was the job I was working the day I climbed down the manhole on the 59th Street Bridge and took a dangle over the East River.

Still, most of the time, I was broke. It was a good thing I was broke most of the time, because if I hadn't been broke and riding the buses back and forth from my jobs to the college, and from the college to my Mom's house, I wouldn't have run into Ron D. Wayley at the N41 bus stop one cold day in late 1984.

Ron D was part of a DJ Crew called the Play Hard Crew, and he was still riding the bus, too, naw'mean? All of us who were DJ-ing back in the day sort of knew each other.

So Ron says to me, "What's up with your boy, Chuckie D? He swear he nice. I want to battle him."

It was a challenge, straight up.

"Chuck don't swear he nice. He *knows* he nice," I said. "And we don't battle. We'll set you up for a battle, if you want one."

We didn't battle, though battles were a big part of the MC/DJ circle. Chuck D always held himself a little outside of that game. Partly, I think, because if you don't battle, you can't be beat!

Which is where you folks came in.

So Chuck takes my narration and writes some lyrics and we put out "Public Enemy #1" in 1985.

We played "Public Enemy #1" on my show, and it was hot. Real hot. Before long, people were asking for it on the commercial radio stations, too, and it was getting play all over New York. Everyone was asking about the song "Public Enemy #1" and wanting to know where to get that shit.

DMC and Jam Master J called. We knew them because we'd had them on our show. The next thing you know, they were meeting with Chuck, talking about that single and what to do with it to get it released everywhere. Run's brother, Russell Simmons, had started Def Jam Recordings with Rick Ruben and was still managing Run's group. DMC and Jam Master J were there to convince Chuck to sign with the label and put "Public Enemy #1" out on a record. My old buddy, Bill Stephney, was now working with Def Jam, too, and he really wanted to see us get on the label and get that record out, too.

Def Jam wasn't doing that well. Def Jam had started in 1983 and it was struggling for a second, even though it had already gotten a distribution deal with CBS Records and their music was getting around. Still, their rep wasn't all that great then.

They were signing people, but the artists weren't getting their just due. We knew it. The community of hip hop was small then, and you heard exactly what was going on. Def Jam had two major artists, LL Cool J and *The Beastie Boys* and, like I said, their records were getting played, but the guys making the music weren't seeing the money they were supposed to see, naw'mean? Chuck wasn't sure he wanted to sign with Def Jam, since it didn't seem like their reputation was that good. He listened to what DMC and J had to say, but he didn't just jump on the deal. He waited a while, thinking it over.

Good move, Gee.

'Cause while he was thinking, LL Cool J went platinum with his "BAD" (Bigger and Deffer) album, and then *The Beastie Boys'* "License to Ill" went platinum. Then Oran "Juice" Jones came out with "The Rain" that went to near the top of the R&B charts. Def Jam signed a girl named Allyson Williams, who put out a single called, "Just Call My Name" and—you got it, platinum. Allyson Williams, that's my girl, Gee! Whassup, Allyson? I love you! I'm still here and I haven't went nowhere!

So now, Def Jam is making money and they finally start treating their artists right, making sure they get paid the right amounts on time and shit. Chuck D decides to sign, but there is a problem, folks. A problem called "Flavor Flav."

Def Jam wanted to sign Chuck D, but they didn't want your boy, Flav.

They said my voice was high, peaky and annoying. They said the style for rap was a low, bass sounding voice. I didn't sound like that, and since I didn't, they didn't think I added anything to the group.

Chuck went to Russell and Rick Ruben, who were running Def Jam then, and he told them, "I won't do this without my partner. It's Flavor that *makes* the record 'Public Enemy #1.' Without him, it's just another rap record."

That, ladies and gentlemen was the beginning of *Public Enemy*, and how Chuck D forced your boy Flavor Flav down Def Jam's throat, which ended up being one of the biggest things that ever happened to Def Jam and to music. I brought something to the table that they needed. Not only was I part of a rap group that was bringing black power and social consciousness into the game, but I was also straight from the street, straight from the hood, and straight from catburglarland. I *was* the life they were rapping about. I wasn't a college boy like Hank and Chuck, not that there's anything wrong with that. I wasn't a student of the politics of black disenfranchisement or no shit like that, either. I was a straight up nigga from the 'hood. I'd done drugs, run numbers, and been to jail. I wasn't perpetrating a street style. I *was* the street.

People knew it, too. They felt it. They vibed it.

I became one of the most sampled voices in the history of music. Nobody's voice has ever been sampled more than Flavor Flav's, to this day. James Brown used to be the most sampled voice until I came along with "Yeah Boy" and "Rock that shit, homey." That took James Brown's record and stripped it nekkid! The things I said hyping *Public Enemy* were part of street language, which people today call "ebonics." How in the hell is someone gonna take my street language and give it a corny-ass name like "ebonics?"

Anyway, that's what I brought to the table and that's what Simmons and Rubin didn't understand at that meeting when Chuck D signed.

I am the one who brought street language into records.

I brought the 'hood into rap music.

I'm the First Nigga of street records. There were no other street niggas on motherfucking records until me.

Nobody does the street nigga better than me, naw'mean?

Yeah, I'm a nigga and I'm proud to be one, but don't call me "nigger," 'cause that's something different. If you say, "Yo, Flav, my nigga, what's happenin'?" Then, I'm gonna respond and we're cool, but if you call me "nigger" I'm gonna say, "Pull my trigger, suck my dick and make it bigger."

And I'm gonna wanna fight.

Hee,hee, har, har!

Naw'mean?

Chuck D, Hank Boxley and I signed with Def Jam in late 1985 as the group *Public Enemy*. Hank named the group *Public Enemy* from that first single, "Public Enemy #1," which was released nationally in 1986. Our first album, "Yo Bum Rush the Show," came out a year later, in 1987.

It was Chuck D who started calling me "Flavor Flav" right around the time that first single came out. The name didn't really take off and become popular until "It Takes a Nation of Millions to Hold Us Back," our second album, hit in 1989. That's when I started using it in shows and calling myself "Flavor Flav!" The rest, folks, is history!

Chapter 3

Flavor Flav
Gets Clocked

I'M STANDING IN THE WINGS of the Capitol Theatre in Passaic, New Jersey, waiting to go on stage and perform. From what I can tell, all 3,200 seats in the place have a butt in them. Not that they're sitting in their seats, though. They're hyped, man. They're on their feet. They're ready, man.

And so am I, yo.

It's the *Beastie Boys* they came to see, but *Public Enemy* is opening for them on one of the legs of their "License to Ill" tour. It is our first concert as a group, part of a tour with the *Beasties* that's gonna help get us out there before our first album comes out. In a matter of seconds, I'm gonna step out on that stage and do my thing.

Before that night, people had heard Flavor on the single "Public Enemy #1," but hardly anyone outside of Roosevelt or Freeport, Long Island had ever seen me. I could have looked any way I wanted to, and I was wearing a shower clock around my neck.

"What you got that thing on for?" my group wanted to know.

"You gonna take that off, right?"

Nope.

I went right out on that stage with that shower clock around my neck, and did my thing, naw'mean?

It started out as a dare.

See, the night before the show, I was hanging out with some of my friends, like usual. We were sitting in one of the hallways at the projects at 25 Buffalo Avenue in Freeport, playing the dozens, laughing and having a good time, like we always did back then.

There was a lady named Joyce Miller, a crackhead who came through the building selling these shower clocks that she just had just stole from this store called Fortunoff's on Carl Place. You know the kind that you hang from the shower head? Back in the day, they was in, man, and everybody had one of them, or was trying to get one. My boy TA took the stop watch off my neck and put the shower clock around it instead. Everyone in the hallway was dying laughing. I mean, they were rolling on the floor because it looked so funny.

"Yo, Flavor! I dare you to wear this thing around your neck on stage tomorrow night! I dare you, man!" TA said.

Well, let me tell you something. If you dare me to do something, I'm gonna do it. I ain't no pussy, man. I ain't scared.

I took that clock right out of his hands and put it back around my neck at show time.

I haven't taken it off since.

Seriously.

On that first tour with *The Beastie Boys*, my clock became very popular. The dare was done, and I could have taken it off, but I didn't. Chuck D started wearing one, too, because the whole idea of the clock really looked dope.

I kept wearing it. I don't know why, other than it just seemed like a part of the performance, even after the show. I've worn it to every concert since then. I wear it every single day when I leave the house. *Every day*. Most of the time, it's that same clock that my friends dared me to put around my neck the night before *The Beastie Boys'* tour began in Passaic, New Jersey.

Well, maybe not exactly the same one, but the same kind. I bought a whole box of them once on sale. Your boy's like everyone else—Flavor Flav *loves* a bargain!

Hee, hee, har, har!

Of course, I've got all kinds of clocks. Dozens, in fact. Maybe even a hundred. People sometimes give them to me, and I've got fancier versions for events and photographs. Most days, I wear that clock from 1986 everywhere I go. I take it off when I'm at home, but when I go out, I put it right back on.

Now you know what time it is. That's how the clock became my signature piece, but the clock was just part of it.

I started plenty of street lingo and styles, man.

Hair?

I was wearing the high top fade when *Kid 'n' Play* started out. Kid and I had a competition going—a little personal growing match to see who could get their hair the highest. He finally grew his hair so high that I couldn't catch up with him.

Moves?

I'd dance on stage, and every dance I put out in the street caught on and lasted for two years or better. Yeah, your boy used to *put it in*, naw'mean? I put it in, yo.

Clothes?

I started people wearing their hats to the side, and sunglasses at all times of day and night. I am also the one who started everyone in the world wearing bright, florescent colors.

I started wearing high top sneakers with a tuxedo, and now everyone does it. I'm the one that brought the top hat and army boots into hip hop music. Next thing you know, my boy K-Ci (Cedric Hailey) from the group *Jodeci* was doing it. Then everyone started following.

Now I know y'all have heard the expression "Yo, Gee!" That's because I'm the first one to put "Gee" on records. Now I have the whole world calling each other "Gee" like,"Whassup, Gee?" "How you doin', Gee?" "Where's my money, Gee?" and stuff like that.

You gotta remember, folks, I was the first.

I'm even the one who told Tone Loc to use "Cold Medina" in his song. There was this drug addict named Homer Clark that I knew from the streets of Freeport, who used to hang with my father. He used to say it all the time. It's really his phrase, but I started saying it. Tone heard me say it and he asked me, "What's cold medina?" I told him, "It means cold pumpin', no slumpin'. It's the bag you wanna jump in!" I told him, "Hey man, use it and make a record with it!"

Tone Loc made the record "Funky Cold Medina" and it sold 3 million copies. *The Beastie Boys* named the drink "fuzzy navel" the "cold medina."

Hee, hee, har, har, people!

Along with my clock, I'm also known for a two-word phrase.

"Yeeaah boooyyyeee!"

LL Cool J used to say "Yeah boy" all the time, and he got me saying it. You'd say something like, "That's a slamming beat, yo!", and LL would say, "Yeah, boy!" like that. He said it so much, I kinda picked it up. That's how I started saying it, but I had to make it my own, naw'mean? I had to change it up a bit. I took the "yeah" and made it longer and I took the "boy" and I made it longer and let my voice go up a bit at the end.

That's how you got the "YEAAAAHHHHHHH BOOOO YYEEE."

Speaking of LL Cool J, I gotta tell two quick stories about him, folks.

That's one of the reasons why you're reading this book, right? To hear my stories? So check this out:

Just in case you didn't know, LL Cool J's real name is Todd Smith. There are lots of Smiths in America. It's a very common name y'know, but his Smith family is one of a very large group of Smiths from the Shinnecock Indian Reservation in eastern Long Island.

Now here's the freaky part, folks.

My father's mother, your boy's grandmother, Estella Maude Smith, was *also* a Smith from the Shinnecock Reservation!

By LL being a Smith and my grandmother being a Smith, I have a feeling folks, that somewhere along the line me and LL Cool J might be related! He might be my blood cousin or something.

See the resemblance?

Hee,hee, har, har!

I will take time one day to seek this out and find out if we're cousins for real, man. Even if we're not, I want to say thanks to LL Cool J for "Yeeaah boooyyyeee" because it made me the most sampled voice in the history of music.

Now, if I find out that we *are* cousins then—whassup, cuz!

Hee, hee, har, har!

So that's one LL Cool J story. Here's another one:

Once me and LL Cool J went to shoot this video for a group Jam Master J was involved with called *The Afros*. The song was "Feel It" off their album "Kicking Afrolistics," and there's a shot of me coming up out of the swimming pool with a bottle in my hand, my ball cap on sideways and my big white sunglasses. If you look close, there's also a shot of me dancing the Soul Train line with a big Afro wig on my head, too! It was like a party, doing that video, and after it was over, I brought LL to my neighborhood projects so he could meet everybody.

By "everybody," I was thinking my family and like that, but he ended up meeting almost the entire 'hood, naw' mean?

Man, the whole the projects came out to see him. I mean, the people went *crazy*. I took him to my cousin, Missy Ladsen's, house. Just about everybody in the building was crammed into her little apartment, and the rest of the city was outside in the street. I was happy to bring some excitement to my neighborhood, naw'mean? This was 1990, when LL Cool J was big and I was on my way to being big, too.

People had started to identify me by the clock, the glasses, and the energy I put into every single performance. By the time our second album, "It Takes a Nation of Millions to Hold Us Back," came out, *Public Enemy* was getting pretty well known. By the time "Welcome to the Terrordome" and

"Apocalypse 91...The Enemy Strikes Black" came out, everybody was talking about us.

I'm known as the greatest "hype man" ever and anyone who knows me knows it's a role I was born to play. I been a "hype man" my whole life.

People come up to me in the street and say "Flav, I love your craziness, man. You make me laugh." Then they want to know whether it's an act or what.

Well...

Yo, you gotta turn the page, Gee.

Chapter 4

Hype or Hyper?

Picture being in a classroom, right? Around 1970 or 1971.

Lots of desks lined up in rows, with the teacher's desk at the front. Her chair is pulled out from the desk a bit and the blackboard is behind it, naw'mean? All the kids are in their seats, their eyes darting to the doorway, where the teacher is leaning out into the hallway talking to another teacher.

A little Flavor Flav is creeping up to the teacher's desk with a handful of tacks in my palm.

Creeping...creeping...

I laid those tacks down in her chair carefully, one near the front, one near the back and one on each side.

I go back to my seat just as the teacher turns back into the room.

"Sit down, Mr. Drayton!" she yells and then goes back to her seat.

Man, you could just see every one of the kids leaning forward to see if she would actually....

"OOWWW!" she screamed, and she jumped up out the seat and started grabbing at her big behind!

The kids just fell out laughing, man, and I just started laughing and falling out all over the floor with them. I mean, she knew I did it because she saw me, but I didn't care. I just kept laughing and letting the classroom love me, naw'mean? Yeah, I got in trouble for it, but I didn't care.

Hee, hee, har, har!

That happened when I was in the fourth or fifth grade. I probably was about ten, I guess. I attended Leo F. Giblyn School from kindergarten to fourth grade, then I moved over to Carolyn G. Atkinson School for the fifth and sixth grade. Then I went to John W. Dodd Junior High School for seventh and eighth grade. I got left back in the seventh grade, so I spent an extra year there before going to Freeport High School and dropping out in the tenth grade.

But back to the fourth grade and those tacks.

I remember that we were a class full of trouble-makers, man. It wasn't *just* me, but it *was* me a lot of the time. That's because I've always loved to clown around, make people laugh and act crazy. I've been doing crazy shit for as long as I can remember.

At home everything that I touched broke. Everything. It wasn't always my fault. Some of that shit was broke long before I got there, but once I touched it, it was broken, man. I don't know how. Everyone hid their stuff from me—my mother, my father, my two older sisters, Gail and Pam. "Don't let Ricco touch it," they'd say. "'Cause if he touches it, you know what's gonna happen."

I got into other kinds of trouble, too.

There was a Nabisco factory in our 'hood, man. We used to break in and steal cookies. Big old boxes of them. Me and my friends used to break in at night and have cookie fights. One night I got hit in the eye with a Nilla Wafer. Damn, that thing hurt! Oreos hurt too, but those Nilla Wafers were the *worst*. You could put someone's eye out with a Nilla Wafer. No joke.

We stole so many cookies. We took them to school and had cookies in our lockers, cookies in our backpacks, cookies everywhere and all over the school.

I'm sure if you could have tested me back then, I'd have been ADHD or ADD or some combination of letters that means you're hyperactive, always running around, and always into something. My teachers hated to see me coming because I was always a hyper kid. I was Dennis the Menace. I was the class crown. I was hyping the class up and getting the crowd pumped for my next antic.

Sure, I got punished, but I didn't care. I didn't take anything seriously. I used to shoot spit balls at teachers while they were looking me right in the face. Once, I think it was in the first grade, a teacher made me mad so I stood on her desk, punched her in her face, jumped down and ran out.

I got suspended, and that might have been the first time, but it wasn't the last.

I got paddled. They used to do that then—beat your ass with a great big paddle with holes in it. It looked kind of like a waffle. I got whacked on the butt so damn hard with that paddle that my butt would be red and sore for days.

Yeah boy. Me and the paddle were pretty intimate with each other. Me and the paddle became really good friends.

Speaking of friends, I had partners in mischief. My friends were Barry and Garry Mosley, and Enoch Massey (who we called Lil Jimmy), and my two cousins Marsha and Chris. There were also the two Davids—David Gillem and David Higgs. Getting into trouble is partly peer pressure, folks. They do stuff and you do stuff too, when you're with them, including some really dumb, daredevil-type stuff.

Like when we used to walk on the Long Island Railroad train tracks, and take rocks and line them up on the rails. The heavy wheels of the trains would either crush them or send them flying. Once we put a really big rock on the tracks and derailed the train. The first car jumped off the track and we all ran. No one was really hurt, but train service was delayed for hours while they got that car out of the way.

We were 'bout eight when we did that.

Sometimes, we went to Freeport where the train yard was, where the trains would park at the end of the day. We'd go up there and start the trains up and drive them down the tracks. We'd get them goin' good, then jump off and the train would keep on going...

And going...

And going...

As far as I know, no one ever got hurt from that either.

I stole a LIRR train once and drove it from Freeport to the nearby town of Merrick. I shit you not. I did it, then jumped off, onto the platform in Merrick and watched the train go down the track by itself, with no one driving it.

Why?

So I would have some good shit to tell you about in this book!

Hee, hee, har, har!

I was the kid playing on the railroad tracks, throwing metal pipes at the third rail.

Yeah, boy, that was me and my friend Garry, throwing a metal pipe at the third rail, trying to see what would happen. Garry backed out after a bit because he got spooked, man, but me? Nah, I was determined. I was gonna see what would happen when that metal hit the third rail. I tried the first time and closed my eyes, but it missed and nothing happened. I went and got the pipe and I tried again, closing my eyes in case it hit, but it didn't. It missed again. On the third try, I threw it, but this time I didn't close my eyes, because I wanted to see what was going to happen. I threw the pipe and it connected with that third rail, and when it did…

Wooowwww!

It made a spark so big and so bright, I was blinded for a good 40-50 seconds. That's a long time to be without your eyesight. I was so dazed by that spark that I barely heard the horn of the oncoming train.

When I finally did hear it, I couldn't figure out which way to run. The train operator was blowing the horn loud and long, but I was just standing there, blinking. The train was coming at me very fast. When I could finally see, I jumped off the tracks and rolled down the hill, just as the train hit the tracks where I had been standing just a few seconds before.

Whew! That was a close call! I told you I've always been a daredevil, and that ain't the half of it.

We used to go train surfing when we were kids, too. I was probably about eight or nine years old. When the train was stopped in the station, we used to climb up on top of it and ride on its roof to the next stop. Those trains would go pretty fast, maybe 60 miles per hour, and they went through all kinds of tunnels where you'd have to lay flat or you'd smash your head against the stones of a bridge and kill yourself quick. Man, I almost smashed into those tunnels so many times! Even though I didn't smash, many times I scraped my back on the tunnel roof or fell off the roof and slid over the side of the moving train, hanging off the side.

I should have been scared, but I wasn't. I kept doing it.

Bus surfing? Yeah, we did that too. You stand on the rear bumper of the bus and hold on to the grooves on the rear window and ride a few stops. I got caught by a Nassau County police officer once doing that on the N4 bus on the way to Freeport High School. The officer pulled his gun on me and shouted, "Get down!"

I jumped off and ran.

We used to stack up three regular mattresses and jump off the two-story roof onto them. I had to outdo my friends, so I jumped, did a flip, hit the mattress and then bounced off of it, hitting the ground. It knocked the wind out of me, and my back was messed up, Gee.

That wasn't first time that your boy did a roof jump. I did the Mary Poppins with an umbrella and jumped off a four story building, the projects at 20 Albany Avenue, when I was five. Yeah, I was only five and I thought that if Mary could do it, so could your boy, Flav!

I opened up the umbrella and I took a leap for mankind. It worked a little bit. By the time my feet got to the top of the third floor window, the umbrella broke and I fell three stories down to the ground. Luckily, I landed in some bushes and grass.

That time, I broke an arm and a leg.

I was back on the rooftop in no time, though, sitting there with my legs dangling from it. No more, Mary Poppins for me, but to this day, I love the sensation of flying.

I wasn't afraid of nothing. Although I've gotten busted up a few times, I've never gotten hurt badly enough to stop me from trying anything. While I still ain't scared, I wouldn't take those chances now. I have lot hanging over my head now. A lot of people that I take care of besides just myself. These days, I'm trying *not* to get hurt, physically or mentally. Mental pain can be worse than physical pain. A lot worse. There's a lot of people that I know today who hurt so much mentally, they *wish* for physical pain. Mental and emotional pain can kill you quick, for real. These days, I tried to stay away from pain of any kind.

When I was young, though, I was a thrill seeker and a clown. If it would give my friends a laugh, or make a good story, I did it.

At the age of nine, I hotwired and stole my first car. I watched the older boys do it, then I went and tried it and it worked, so I started doing it all the time. I'd hotwire a car and go joyriding. License? Who needs a license? If your legs are long enough to reach the pedals and you can see over the steering wheel, you can drive, folks.

You remember that car bodywork place, Maaco? Well, people would take their cars to Maaco to get them painted, but me and my friends used to break into the Maaco lot, hotwire the cars and play a real-life game of bumper cars or crasharoos! Uh oh, better get Maaco!

Construction sites? Man, you know it. Those construction workers would leave the keys in the trucks, the cranes and tractors and we'd go at night and drive the equipment around town.

I stole cranes, trains, cars, and tractors. If it rolled, I stole it and took it for a ride.

I was like that at school, too.

I already told you about the tacks in the fourth grade. I had to repeat the seventh grade because of clowning around and cutting school. I could make the class laugh, but I didn't do my work. Of course, there was marijuana. By then, I'd discovered weed, and I'd go to class so high that all I could do was lay my head on the desk. I'd be sleeping and snoring and the whole nine during classes. The only thing that woke me up was the bell to go to the next period. When I woke up, I always had something funny to say to put the class in stitches.

When people ask me about hyping and about where I learned to do what I do on stage, what can I say? My life is clowning and risk-taking. It's what I've always done. If I weren't doing it on stage for *Public Enemy*, I'd be doing it in some kind of way, no matter what.

That ain't no "character" or "alter ego." It's just me.

Chapter 5

Flavor Flav Prefers the Tour Bus

I'M SITTING ON AN AIRPLANE, and I am one nervous Gervis. Nervous, but not scared, naw'mean?

I have never been on a plane before, but now *Public Enemy* is performing at the Fox Theatre in Detroit with *The Beastie Boys* and I'm gonna fly.

So me, Chuck D and Hank go over to LaGuardia Airport and board a Northwest flight. I'm sitting by the window and as that big bird jumped up into the air, my heart felt like it left my body, crashed through the plane's walls and hit the ground, man. It was hard for me to breathe, naw' mean? I felt almost like I'd been dunked in ice water or something. It was awful, but once my feet were back on the ground, I couldn't wait to do it again.

Hee, hee, har, har!

I fell in love with flying on that first flight, and to this day, I love it. I really want to thank God for all the successful flights I've taken. There are a lot of people who got on an airplane for the first time and didn't make it off to talk about it. I've been around the world two and a half times, and to almost every state in the United States at least once, and I've never had more than a few bumpy rides along the way.

Of course, every time I take off, I say my own special little prayer to God and I thank Him every time I have a safe landing. Prayer is a part of my life, man. Seriously. *Public Enemy* prays before we go out on stage at every show. Actually, we pray two prayers. One is *The Lord's Prayer* that I lead myself. Then, one of the S1Ws, Pop Diesel or Brother James, leads a second prayer. I'm sure prayer is one of the reasons that *PE* has remained successful for so long.

I'm supposed to be telling you about taking Flavor Flav out on the road as a major part of *Public Enemy*, one of the most significant rap groups *ever*. We built that reputation not just with our sound and our lyrics, which were unlike anything anyone else had ever done, but also with our stage show. We were touring before our first album, "Yo, Bum Rush the Show," even came out. By the time "It Takes a Nation of Millions to Hold Us Back" came out, everybody was talking about us. Everyone was coming to the shows, man, and everyone wanted to see your boy, Flavor Flav, doing my thing—rocking the mike, doing my dance, and swinging my clock.

Def Jam may not have understood what I brought to the group when Chuck D made them sign me, but the people did. At every show that I did, and every show that I do, even now, they loooovee some Flavor Flav!

Back in 1986 and 87, when we were just getting started, there were some people out there who were kinda confused by us. First, there was this pro-black, militant group with our S1Ws (Security of the First World) on the stage toting fake Uzis. Then there I was, dancing around with a clock around my neck. For some people, that was like, "What the fuck?" Even Howard Stern was confused, and he's also from Roosevelt!

"They're from Roosevelt. I'm from Roosevelt! What's 'tough' about Roosevelt?" he said or something like that.

This was before he was as large as he is now, but he was getting a following. Some of my group didn't like that shit he said, but in the end, it got more and more people talking about us and more curious about our music, so it was cool with me.

I've been on Howard's show a bunch of times since then, and Howard doesn't mess with me, man. You know why? I know how to play the dozens, too—been doing it my whole life, naw'mean? He can't out-snap me, man. I beat him every time. I'm also proud to say that me and Howard became good friends. The last time I was on his show, I was with Brigitte Neilson while we were doing *Strange Love*. Howard had me appear at the beginning of his movie, *Private Parts*. I want to say to Howard, thanks for putting me in the movie, and for becoming my friend. He is one of the most powerful-est people in radio today and no one can take him down! I'm proud of you, Howard.

In the late 1980s and the early 1990s, Howard Stern wasn't the only one talking. Man, everyone was talking about us. We were bringing in something new, something really out there. It was kind of Nation of Islam, Five Percenter philosophy mixed in with social commentary, with all the truth about what was going on in black communities. We talked about politics, the police, AIDS, drugs, and jail—everything and anything that the black community was dealing with.

We were touring with everybody. We did a bunch of cities with *The Beastie Boys'* "License to Ill" tour, then hooked up with *Heavy D and the Boys* for their "Nitro Tour '89," which also featured L.L. Cool J, Big Daddy Kane, Slick Rick, De La Soul and EPMD.

We toured around the world with LL Cool J twice. Then, we went on the *Run DMC* tour back when they had that record, "Run's House." You know that one, it goes, "Who's house? Run's house!" I used to hang out with Run, Jam Master J,

Smith, Garfield, Special Agent E, and Big D. All those guys were part of *Run DMC* or were under Rush Management's umbrella. Rush Management was one of Russell Simmons' companies.

I became good friends with that whole clan, and when they were on stage, somewhere on that stage you'd find Flavor Flav, too.

My group didn't like it, but they couldn't stop me. Run and those guys were my friends.

There was this time when Run DMC was performing and I was on stage, too. I went up on Jam Master J's platform and I accidentally made a record skip. Jam Master J yelled at me, "Hey, what you doing up here?"

He told Runny Ray, his assistant, "Hey, get this guy out of here!"

He said to me, "Don't *ever* come up here again, man. You're making my record skip. I don't like that!"

But hey, your boy has a short memory.

So it was about three days later, all right? I had to tell J something and I went up on his platform again during the show. I'm like tip toeing...tip toeing...trying my best not to make the record skip, but I made the record skip again.

Yo, when it skipped that second time, I remember J reaching for me. I think he wanted to punch me in the face, but he got nothing but thin air, man. I wasn't there. When J reached for your boy, Flavor Flav, I did the Harry Houdini and I was not at the end of his reach! I kept away from his platform after that, though.

I remember being with my group on the bus overseas, which we shared with Run and the crew. In those days, pause button tapes were the thing. When you're touring, there's a lot of down time when you're just riding between one city and the next one, and when you're in Europe man, it's riding between countries, too. Me and Jam Master J used to sit on the back of the bus, having a contest of who could make the best pause button tape.

All you needed was some music and a decent cassette or CD player with a pause button. You play the tune and you pause it to create a different rhythm, which makes it like a loop, naw'mean?

Mine was always the best. I was always killing Jam Master J in the contest, but you know J. He always had to be the winner.

Why?

Because he was Jam Master J, that's why! I ain't mad at him!

I really feel that's where J came up with the platinum record called "Pause," which was on *Run DMC's* fifth album, "Back from Hell," in 1989. I think he got the idea while he was sitting on the back of the bus with me, doing those pause button tapes, killing time on that 1988 tour we did together.

Man, Jam Master J!

I love and miss him so much, naw'mean?

Speaking of missed, I'd known Tupac Shakur since he was 16 years old.

Back in the days when *Public Enemy* and *Digital Underground* used to tour together, in the early 1990s, Tupac was more like a roadie than a member of the band, naw'mean? He did a little background stuff with *Digital Underground*, but they really didn't let him get on the mike that much. After the shows, Tupac, my nephew Ronald (who we called "Rondu") and I would hang out all the time.

Once, out on the tour, someone stole the S1W's plastic Uzis. I remember us all running around backstage, trying to find out who did it. We found the guy and we took him in the dressing room, and Tupac took off his belt and started whipping the guy's ass, like he was child. It was funny, man. Then, everyone took a punch at him for stealing our stuff.

I was getting crazy—you know, your boy, Flavor Flav, can get a little crazy—so I went and grabbed the fire extinguisher. I raised it over my head, ready to hit the guy over the head with it, and Tupac snatched it out of my hand. He pushed me hard up against the wall and said, "What are you, crazy? You wanna kill him? Over a plastic Uzi?"

I wasn't thinking. I was just crazy and caught up in the moment, I guess. I didn't know the fire extinguisher would have killed him.

Tupac stopped me from committing a murder.

That would have been really bad, man. The tour would have ended, the audience would have had to go home, and I would have gone to jail.

That's a story that a lot of people don't know. I was about to do something really stupid, and Tupac stopped me. Actually, God stopped me and he used Tupac to do it.

Life is deep, man. Wowww...

Stuff like that used to go on backstage all the time. Once, *Public Enemy, Houdini*, Queen Latifah, Slick Rick and Big Daddy Kane were touring together, and Slick Rick and Big Daddy Kane got into it. We were back stage and Big Daddy Kane walked up to Slick Rick and they were arguing and all that. Then Big Daddy Kane punched Slick Rick right in the eye patch.

I mean, come on, folks. Have a heart! Punch the guy in the good eye, not the bad eye!

Big Daddy Kane didn't have a heart that night, not at all.

Lyor Cohen was there and he came running over to me after the fight.

"Flavor, Flavor! They are fighting! You have to stop this."

I remember looking at him like, "What you want *me* to do about it?"

"Everybody will listen to you, Flavor!" Lyor said in his funny accent.

Right, Flavor the mediator. Sure.

But okay, Lyor.

I took the two aside. We went into a room and talked. Next thing you know, Big Daddy Kane and Slick Rick shook hands, and that's the way we did it.

Like I said, stuff was always happening back stage. But back to 'Pac.

We were in Manhattan last time I saw him, and there was an event down by the Hudson River. I'd heard he was having beefs with all kinds of different people and I'll never forget that, when I snuck up on him to surprise him, he almost punched me in the face! He thought I was someone else.

Two years later, when Tupac was shot and killed, I was very sad. That took a big chunk out of me because me and Tupac were very good friends. That was the last thing I would have expected to hear had happened to him.

Queen Latifah used to help babysit my kids on another tour. Yeah, that's right. The Queen herself, looking out for Flavor Flav's young ones.

That was in 1991, when we all toured together in a show that included *Naughty By Nature*, DJ Jazzy Jeff and the Fresh Prince, DJ Quik, *Heavy D and the Boyz*, MC Lyte, Son of Bazerk, and NSC Daban. Only Shanique and William, Jr. ("Man" he's called in the family) were out on the road with me then. Baby Karren was at home with her mother.

Yeah, *Kid 'n' Play* used to watch the kids for me, too. How about *that*?

Oh...y'all didn't know I had kids? Well, they're a big part of the making, breaking and re-creating of Flavor Flav. I'll get to them in a while, I swear. I always try to get my kids involved in anything I'm doing, man, and my book is no exception.

I don't care what you have read, what you have heard on the radio, or what you thought you saw on TV, I'll tell you straight up—your boy, Flavor Flav, has lots of faults, but I've always tried to keep my kids around me. I've always tried to be a good father. I love my kids, man. All seven of 'em— Shanique, William Jr., Karren, Da'Zyna, Quanah, Kayla and Karma.

But for now, back to the music.

In the end, *Public Enemy* became one of the most power- ful-est rap groups in the history of music. In 2009, *Rolling Stone* named us one of the top 100 most influential groups in music history, as the best rap group of all time, and our single, "Fight the Power," as the best rap record of all time. We were the first rap group on the cover of *Ebony* magazine, along with *Salt-n-Pepa*. In the article, we were right there above the picture of Will Smith when he was the Fresh Prince with DJ Jazzy Jeff!

We weren't just fighting the power, we were *using* it, too.

In the late 1980s, when the federal government made Martin Luther King's birthday a holiday, a handful of states weren't with the program. Arizona was one of them. After

Coretta Scott King, Stevie Wonder and a bunch of other people got together in protest, most entertainers decided to put pressure on the state to honor the holiday by boycotting. Yeah, boy, wasn't nobody performing in Arizona.

Chuck D wrote a protest record called "By the Time I Get to Arizona" that was included on the "Apocalypse '91" album. Then, *Public Enemy* went out on tour with *U2* on their "Zoo TV Tour" after the release of their album "Achtung, Baby," and one of the stops was in Tempe, Arizona. Well, that put us in a dilemma. We were contracted to tour, but we wanted to honor the boycott. Chuck D got a brilliant idea.

We did the concert, but we came out on stage in total silence. We did the "black power salute"—you know, the single fist raised in the air, made famous by Tommie Smith and John Carlos at the 1968 Olympics in protest of human rights violations against people of color around the world. Then Terminator X (Norman Rogers) started the record and we performed "By the Time I Get to Arizona." When the song was over, we got quiet, gave them the black power salute again, then turned around and walked off the stage.

Wowww! The crowd was *heated*. A lot of people were mad because they wanted to hear more from us, and they felt like they hadn't gotten their money's worth. There were a lot of other people who understood the protest and they teamed up with all the people who were working to get that holiday celebrated in Arizona. The following year, Arizona started recognizing Dr. Martin Luther King's birthday as a holiday and a national day of service. Part of the reason why is what *Public Enemy* did when we played in Tempe in 1992.

That's a musical accomplishment, folks.

I loved touring, and I loved touring with *The Beastie Boys*. I had fun with the group *U2*. You have to remember, I'd gone from playing the parks in Roosevelt, where a good turnout was a few thousand people, to playing in stadiums of 65,000 and 70,000 people! All of them loved some Flavor Flav! It gave me a big rush, but opening up for *U2* was definitely one of the heights of my life, man. I would love to work with Bono and Edge again.

PE was at its peak then, but even though we were riding high professionally, we had *lots* of problems behind the scenes.

On that first tour with *The Beastie Boys* in 1986, they had a tour bus. It was giiiiiii-gantic, yo! Eeeeee-normous. The flyest motherfuckin' tour bus you can imagine.

Me, Chuck, Terminator and the rest of the group didn't have no tour bus. We had an old white, six-passenger van. Now think about it. You can either ride from city to city with five other dudes in a van, or join the headliners in their nice, comfortable, luxurious tour bus. What would *you* do?

Well, you know what I did.

Tour bus. I got on stage with them, too.

I liked *The Beastie Boys*, man. I liked them and became

friends with them. Yeah, I was the only black dude on the stage with a bunch of white boys, slipping and sliding around in Budweiser beer, but I had fun.

My group hated it.

I guess they felt like, since we were a pro-black group, I should have stayed with the black people. I went where I felt like I wanted to go, man. *The Beastie Boys* were making music and having fun, and they had that huuuu-mongous tour bus!

Hee, hee, har, har!

You would think my group would have been happy that I was riding in the tour bus. It made for more room for them in that little van, right, Gee? But, no. They were pissed about it, and they let me know.

Then there were the hotels. Chuck D was my roommate at first, but *that* didn't last too long. I mean, we had two completely different lifestyles, man. Chuck didn't like smoking or drinking. In fact, the group stated itself to be completely against that stuff, so Chuck, Griff, Hank and Norm, they didn't smoke or drink. But me...

Well, your boy liked to find where the party was. I used to hang out late, smoke, drink and get high. I'd come stumbling in the room after a show, sometimes four or five in the morning, and Chuck would be pissed. He hated it. He hated that I woke him up, but I think he hated it more because he just didn't want me doing that stuff.

We weren't roommates for long.

In 1987, when we first toured Europe for LL Cool J's *Radio* tour—that was when he had the record "I Can't Live Without My Radio" and we were out there opening for him—after our set, my group would leave the stage. I'd leave with them, but not for long. No, before long, your boy would pop out on stage during LL Cool J's set.

Chuck and Griff would be like, "Why do you gotta go on someone else's set? Stay out of their set."

"If they say I can hang out on stage with them, then I'm gonna go do it," I said.

And I did.

No matter what they said, I did what I wanted to do anyway. I'm glad that I listened to myself and not to anyone else. They wanted to hold me back, but I didn't want to just belong to *PE*. I wanted to belong to everybody.

If I had listened to them, and if I'd stayed in the groove they wanted me to be in, I wouldn't be the iconic figure I am today.

Things started to get more and more heated between us. I felt like they couldn't stand me because here I was, a black man, in a pro-black rap group, and I was hanging out in the tour bus with the white boys.

Or because I liked to be on stage, hyping and supporting the other artists.

Or because they stood for a lifestyle free from alcohol and drugs, and I did both.

Yeah, they shitted on me because of that.

If anything, they should have been trying to take care of me and trying to get me some help because, by the early 1990s, my drug use was out of control, but they didn't do shit. Not even when I fell off a motorbike while we were touring in Italy and broke both my arms. Would those motherfuckas lift a finger to help me carry a bag?

Hell, no.

That time, I found this girl named Pauwla to help me lug my stuff from the bus to the hotel and back the whole time we were in Italy. She did a lot for me—wiped my nose and wiped my ass. She did a lot and I'm really grateful. Thank you, Pauwla, for helping me out. Wherever you are, I would love to hear from you and see you again!

As for my group? Those motherfuckas just watched. I had two broken arms, but they put a headset on my head and made me do the show anyway, and still wouldn't help me with my bags. Yep, they really shitted on your boy that trip.

By now, my group knew about my drug problem.

At the beginning, when we first signed with Def Jam, they didn't know. No one really knew, not even Karren Ross, the girl I was living with at the time. More on Karren, later. Right now, I'm talking about my group, naw'mean? They didn't know I was strung out. They knew I used, but they didn't know how bad it was getting.

It was getting real bad for your boy, but I'll tell you one thing I know for sure—if I hadn't been using as much as I was, I probably would have killed Professor Griff.

I'm not kidding.

I probably would have shot him and gone to jail for life, if it hadn't been for drugs.

Here's the reason why...

Chapter 6

How Drugs Kept Your Boy *Out* of Jail

O NE NIGHT, I WENT TO THE studio at 510 South Franklin Avenue to meet up with the group.

I was late, really late, naw'mean? I might have smoked a bit, and I'm not talking about cigarettes, though I might have smoked a few them, too. I'm talking about crack cocaine, mixed with weed.

Okay, so I'd been out having a good time, and I'm feeling good, but now I'm coming to the studio to get to work with my group. I had my boom box with me—everyone walked around with their boom box then—and I was playing music as I walked into the lobby of the studio.

Professor Griff yanked my box out of my hands and smashed it on the ground. Before I could say, "What the hell are you doing?" he kicked me in the ribs and in my shin bone, fracturing both.

Your boy went down. I mean, I went down *hard*.

Griff does martial arts and shit, and me, Flav, I'm a buck fifty soaking wet. A couple of the guys picked me up off the floor and somehow I got to my car and drove off. I had so much animosity and hate built up for this guy because of what he did to me. Most of all, he destroyed my feelings.

I gotta tell you, when Griff did that shit to me, I became very, very angry. I was shocked, too. I couldn't believe he'd do something like that. I thought we were cool. I thought we were friends. He never apologized, and I really wanted to pay him back.

I wanted to see him dead.

I'm serious.

We were working on "Yo, Bum Rush the Show" and I would come to the studio with a gun on me. If Griff had even made a move in my direction, I would have shot him at close range, no errors.

Once when were all together and Griff got too close to me, I almost did it. I had my gun in my pocket, my finger on the trigger and the safety was off. I was gonna step away from him, pull it out and shoot him.

I didn't do it. I said to myself, "If I kill this man, my whole career goes down the drain. I'll do life, and I won't get to see my baby."

Yeah, Karren was expecting my first child then, and I'm gonna get to that, but back to the story.

I'm telling you—I was *this close* to putting a permanent hole in Griff—*this close*, but I didn't do it. I really thank God for the power of thought, because at the end of the day, everything you do has a result. If you can't take the weight of the result, then don't do it. I knew the result wasn't something that I wanted to take. I knew that God was trying to give me a good life by allowing me to become a rap music star, so I thank God for keeping me from shooting Griff. If I had, I wouldn't be here right now, talking about it and writing about it. I would have been locked up for the rest of my life.

That was just the beginning of how bad things got between me and Griff. As time went by, they got worse. He even jumped on me again on the world tour we did with LL Cool J. It was in Vienna, and once again, he did a roundhouse kick to my jaw, fracturing it. I hit the ground right in front of LL Cool J, then Griff jumped on top of me and started to finish me off. Brother Mike and Pop Diesel, the S1Ws on that tour, stopped him.

That was 1990, and it made me feel like I shoulda killed that motherfucka back in the studio when I had the chance.

Chuck D knew about these incidents, but he didn't do anything. Chuck D and Griff were tight. I thought that after Griff kicked me the first time, he should have been out of the group. I mean, I missed a few shows because of drugs, and that was bad, but I never hit nobody. I never brought any violence into the group. Instead of taking a stand against that shit, Chuck D let it go on. He let Griff do that to me to try to keep me under control.

Like they could beat the drugs out of me or something.

It was a power move on their part, thinking that if I was scared of Griff, they'd be able to keep control of me, but I wasn't scared of Griff. I wasn't scared, and it was a daily struggle for me to keep my anger under control. Griff could have been dead—and then where would their power move have gotten them?

You know what saved Griff's life?

The very thing that made him so mad at me in the first place—drugs.

I was so drugged up that it just made me stay inside and away from people, man. Drugs kept me quiet and in the house. They kept me from feeling stuff, which kept me from doing stuff. I was just too strung out to go kill somebody, even someone who'd disrespected me as much as Griff had done. So, drugs kept me out of jail, in a funny way. They kept me too focused on getting them and using them to care about doing stuff like murder.

Drugs kept me from killing, but they cost me a lot, too. When we weren't touring, my group couldn't find me half the time. I'd be in someone's basement, smoking crack. I missed a lot of shows, and I do owe an apology to Chuck D and all the fans who were counting on me. I didn't want to perform with Griff, and I could avoid that by smoking crack.

Chapter 7

The Flavor of Money

OKAY, YO.

I'm telling this story because I promised myself that if I was gonna write a book, I was gonna be straight up, so don't get mad with me.

Public Enemy is a big success, and your boy is making money. Making money means, the good life, naw'mean?

I'm a bit high and I get this idea:

"Yo, Flav? Why not hop a jet over to Paris, get a few girls and have a party?"

I check my pockets. I've got a rock of crack in one, and a few thousand dollars in the other. I jump in my lime green Corvette—yeah, boy! A lime green Corvette!—and go to LaGuardia.

I get me a ticket and hop on a plane—no luggage, just me, that crack rock, a stem and some weed. A few hours later, I'm in Paris.

I get a hotel room, and then I take a walk.

I walk and I pick up some girls.

Five of them. I don't speak French, man, but the stuff I had in my pockets spoke for me. Language is not an obstacle, naw'mean?

I take the girls to my room and we all get naked. I'm sitting in a chair while one girl is sucking my dick, and another girl is licking my balls. I'm fingering another two, and that fifth one, she's holding my pipe while I'm smoking and kissing her.

I'm in heaven, naw'mean? Flavor Flav is living every man's dream. Crack and weed was good. It was the fucking bomb, you know? But having those girls *do* me while I was lifted? That was the ULTIMATE.

There were times when I did the same thing in Manhattan, or Los Angeles, or wherever else I was. That's how those drugs had me. Yeah, they had me.

While I was high, I didn't waste any time thinking about how much I hated that motherfucka, Griff.

I used to be so strung out sometimes that I'd leave my Corvette in the street, doors hanging open, while I was held up at someone's house, getting coked up. You could find me, Flavor Flav, *Public Enemy's* hype man, the greatest hype man ever in the game, at a little spot that used to be called Monk's Corner or in the apartments over Bunny's Liquor Store in the Bronx, smoking and smoking and smoking. Me and my friends used to smoke so much crack! Hours and hours were spent smoking. Smoking all day, so Griff could keep breathing air.

Okay, it wasn't just Griff that kept me smoking.

I smoked because I liked it.

I smoked because I could afford it.

I smoked because it kept people who I thought were my friends around me.

I smoked because I couldn't stop smoking, even though I don't think I knew that then.

I also smoked because even though *Public Enemy* had caught fire and we were making bank, that shit with Griff, and Chuck's turning a blind eye to it, bugged me out and sent me deeper into drugs, man.

Then, something wonderful happened.

In 1989, Griff did an interview with *The Washington Post*. He said a bunch of stuff about Jewish people that caused a lot of problems for *Public Enemy*. He said that the Jews were responsible for the majority of the evil in the world, and people got *heated!* Then people started saying that "Fight the Power" was anti-Semitic, too, and started going after Spike Lee because he used the song in his movie "Do The Right Thing." People started pulling our records off the shelves in protest.

Smoking crack is *not* a good thing, but at least I wasn't saying things like that and putting the whole group at risk, man.

Griff had to go, or there wasn't gonna be a *Public Enemy* for much longer, naw'mean?

Chuck D didn't want to kick him out even then, but the pressure was on, so he threw him out. For a minute, the whole group disbanded. Then we were re-banded and he was in again. Finally, Griff did something really stupid and started bad-mouthing the group in another article. That was finally it, and he was out of the group for good.

We started working on "Fear of a Black Planet," and that album came out without Griff.

I was glad.

When Griff got kicked out the group, man—well, that was one of the happiest days of my life, naw' mean? The only thing I was mad about was that Chuck D hadn't put him out long before that.

Griff was telling people he didn't like me because of his beliefs. He was a long time member of the Nation of Islam, but I had been in the Nation, too, for a while. Really, I think that all along Griff was just jealous. He was Minister of Information and all that, but the people didn't love him like they loved me. No matter how much I fucked up, people still loved me, man. Griff hated that.

I had the love, man. I had the position in the group that

he wanted, but he couldn't do what I did. He was a Griff, and not a Flavor Flav. He was trying to be in control, trying to be the man, and trying to take his bullshit out on me.

Seriously, yo, these days, Griff and I are cool. I really regret thinking about killing him. I understand that God didn't put me on this earth to kill people. It's the opposite. He put me here to bring people together in love, peace and harmony. I guess as we get older, we value life more, and we get to understand life and each other more. We learn how to take the past and put it behind us. We learn to live for the future. God gave me the power to forgive, not to forget, and to move forward. There're a lot of things in the past that can help you with the future, but there're a lot of things in the past that can wreck your future, too. Those are the things we must leave behind.

For me, these days, I try to stay away from my past.

Years and years later, when Griff wanted to get back into *Public Enemy*, we had a big meeting about it with a bunch of agents and industry people, trying to put together a world tour. Being a man with a big heart, a man of consideration, a man who wants to do the right thing by people, and a follower of Christ (who said "Love thy enemy"—though I would add "from a distance"), I finally gave in. Griff got back into the group. The thing that allowed me to give in and to let him in was knowing that he didn't have a job, and that he needed to tour with the group to help support his family. Like I said,

God gave me the power to forgive, but not to forget. I forgave my man, even though he never apologized for anything.

We're cool. To this day, when we roll, we roll strong.

Chapter 8

The Flavor of Drugs

MY COUSINS, BARBARA ANN AND JUANITA, were prostitutes, and they thought me and my cousin Christopher Deleston needed a lesson.

A *Scared Straight* kind of lesson. You remember that program? They used to take kids to jail to show them what it was like, so they'd never want to go there.

Barbara Ann and Juanita didn't take us to the jail, though. They took us to a heroin shooting gallery. They wanted us to see what heroin did to people.

We walked into an apartment building, which was very, very raggedy and inside one of the apartments. When they took us in there, man, there were all kinds of weird things going on. One man had a huge swollen leg covered with sores and pus from poking himself with needles. Nasty. Another guy had a huge, swollen arm and no fingers except his thumb and his pinkie. They called him "the human claw." In another room, a lady was shooting dope into the veins in her neck, tapping a syringe that was sticking out of the side of her head. I guess she must have run out veins on her body from years of shooting up.

I gotta tell you folks, I don't scare easy, but that experience really marked me for life, naw'mean? I was really, really scared. I knew I didn't want to have anything to do with a needle. I don't have a needle mark anywhere on my body to this day, and the only needles I've ever had anything to do with were when the doctors stuck me.

Hee,hee, har, har!

One day me and my boy TA, the same TA who introduced me to Chuck D, Hank and Keith much later, were on the roof of the projects in Freeport. He was rolling some stuff and I said, "What's that?"

He said, "Crack. Wanna try it?"

We smoked it.

It gave me a rush to my head. It made me jittery and sweaty, and I didn't like it.

On another day, I tried it again. I got the same rush and the same jitters, but it didn't scare me like it did the first time.

The more I used it, the more I got to like it, naw'mean?

I smoked and I smoked until I was hooked. Boy, did your

boy get hooked. I was strung out on crack a lot of the time, but for a long time, I was secretly hung up on it. I was supposed to be selling it, too, but I started smoking my profit. Then I started smoking other people's profit. Then I was short with money. Then I was hiding out, because I owed money and if I got caught without that cash, I was gonna get fucked up, naw'mean?

When it started out, I was selling more than I was smoking, and ended up the opposite.

I ended up becoming my best customer.

The worst, worst, worst mistake I ever made was ever experimenting with drugs in the first place, which started with marijuana when I was in middle school.

Before that, there were cigarettes and alcohol. My mother and her sisters used to throw parties at my grandmother's house. We kids had to clean up after the party and we would taste the leftover drinks in the glasses. I think I started drinking at about six, man. My sisters started me smoking cigarettes around the same age. They were older by seven and eight years. So they were experimenting with that stuff and they thought it was cute to give me a puff, too. Neither one of them smokes or drinks today, but I still do both.

Thanks a lot, Pam and Gail.

I also want to thank you guys for teaching me about doing the nasty when I was five years old! Wowww...in case you guys had forgotten, I didn't! Check this out, yo!

Pam and Gail were already teenagers by the time I went to kindergarten. And being teenagers, they were into a lot of mischief, naw'mean? When I was five years old, my sisters and their friend, Barbara Sparrow, would get me and Barbara's little sister, Ellen, to do the nasty. Yeah, boyee! I been doing the dirty since was five! I remember thinking it was kinda normal being with a little girl like that, rubbing on her and stuff. When I was six, me and Ellen were both in kindergarten at the Leo F. Giblyn School in Freeport and we were playing inside of some barrels—you know those tunnel-looking things on the playground—and we pulled our pants down. As we were grinding on each other, I popped a boner and that time I could feel the tip of my penis penetrating her for the first time. So, I lost my virginity at six years old, Gee. And also, Ellen was the first girlfriend I ever had. She was the only girlfriend I ever had that could beat me up and make me go back with her when I quit her!

Thanks a lot, Pam and Gail!

Hee, hee, har, har!

But seriously, I know y'all didn't mean no harm.

By middle school, when I was around 12 years old, I was smoking marijuana. Then, back in the day, Quaaludes were the thing. Does anybody even know what a Quaalude *is* anymore?

Hee hee, har, har!

After Quaaludes went out, I did orange tabs of THC and purple haze marijuana. I did "double blotter acid," PCP,

cocaine, and once by accident, I sniffed dope, and hemor-
rhaged from my nose the next day. That was just an accident
because I thought it was coke.

That was long before *Public Enemy*, back when I was making my living as head cook at the Nassau County Courthouse.
Maybe 1980 or 1981? Your boy had just gotten his paycheck,
and I smoked two bags of dust at home, then I decided I'd go
up to the Bronx and get some more. I went out and bought
some more dust. I figured I'd use some and then sell the rest.

I'm sitting in the back of the bus on my way home, and
this girl gets on and we're talking and shit. She had me sniff-
ing this stuff that she said was coke, but I didn't think it felt
right. I mean, I know coke. I had been getting coked for a
while, and it makes you feel *up*—way up. This stuff started
bringing me down, way down.

We got off the bus and went to her apartment. She gave
me more of this stuff, and I started nodding out. I didn't like
it, and I told her I was leaving. She started getting mad and
tried to keep from leaving, but my sixth sense told me to get
the hell out of there. I had figured out what her deal was.
That bitch was trying to rob your boy by giving me dope! I
was fucked up, but I wasn't fucked up enough to let her take
my fucking money. I managed to get home, but then I got
this nose bleed that just wouldn't quit.

The next morning, my dad took me Dr. Joseph's office on
Ocean Avenue in Freeport, across the street from the Free-

port Police Station. The doc put gauze up my nose, making a nose pack to stop the blood. When I laid down, man, that gauze started to slide down my throat and it felt like it was covering up my windpipe, choking me. I stuck my fingers in the back of my throat, got lucky, grabbed a piece of the gauze and pulled it out. I was breathing again, but the rest of the gauze was still stuck up in my head. I counted to three and started ripping the gauze until I got it all out. I just kept pulling, and there was bloody gauze all over the floor. I didn't care what was going to happen, as long as I could get it all out. It took forever, but eventually I got it out.

I always said I wouldn't ever mess with dope (heroin) and here I was bleeding from the nose from it? Your boy did plenty of drugs of all kinds, and except for that one accident with that bitch on the bus, I never did mess with dope. The reason was simple. That was the drug that people used when I was growing up and I'll never forget what I saw it do to people in the community, or to my father and his friends.

I had friends who shot dope and I was around them. There were times when I would tighten the rubber around my friend's arm and watch the vein get big while he sprinkled the dope and a little water in a spoon, cooked it over a lighter, then filled the syringe and stuck it into the big vein. When he'd shoot that stuff, I would always turn away. I tied up the arm, but I turned away. I didn't want to see him do it.

There were times when I was around people who stuck

themselves with a needle and never woke up. The next time I saw them, they were in a suit, in a coffin. I've seen too many of my friends overdose on heroin, but that didn't stop me from using marijuana or cocaine.

When *Public Enemy* was at its peak, I was making crazy money and my drug use went crazy to match. I felt like I couldn't stop myself. I went from a $40 a day habit to a $400 a day habit, and at the end I was going through $2,800 a day. I had a $2,800 a day habit for five or six years. That's a lot of money down the drain! Honestly, that was a lot of drugs, too, folks!

Now, I didn't smoke it all by all myself. I would buy it and some "friends," who were not good for my life, would come over and get high with me. No, they'd come over and steal over half my shit. Then I'd have to go get some more for myself.

These people I thought were my friends really weren't my friends. They came to get me high, so that I could get *them* high, so they could steal all my shit. These were my friends from the neighborhood, from back in the day when I was William Drayton or Ricco. I guess they figured that since I had the money now, they might as well get something out of it. If they were *really* my friends, they would have been trying to stop me, so that instead of wasting money on drugs, I might have had some to come back to the old 'hood and help them out.

Nah, man. They didn't think that way and neither did I. It was all about the moment. I wasn't thinking about the future and neither were they.

They needed to get high, just like I did, so they came and got high, and stole some of my shit to sell or use later.

I guess I should be grateful to them. Those "friends" partying with me and stealing my shit might have saved my life. Maybe if they hadn't stolen my shit from me, those hits might have been the hits that ended my life, so I thank God for those lousy freeloaders stealing my shit. The truth is, the more drugs that were around me at that point, the more drugs I would have done.

Even without those hits, drugs ultimately cost your boy, Flavor Flav, everything he'd built as a member of *Public Enemy*, my first relationship and three of my kids, my second relationship and three more of my kids.

Like going down that manhole and finding myself hanging 180 feet over the East River with nothing to stop me from falling, I was in a hole, man. The deepest, darkest hole I've ever fallen into in my life.

PART TWO

The Breaking of Flavor Flav

Chapter 9

Breaking the Flavor

I WAS FEELING GOOD.

Yeah, I was high, but I felt good and I wanted to keep feeling good. I knew the feeling would wear off soon if I didn't get more drugs.

I had money, Gee. I had crazy money. It was 1997. Things had been rocky with *Public Enemy* and Def Jam, but there was money coming in so I didn't really care much about all that. I had about $800,000 in the bank, even after spending quite a bit—mostly on drugs, but not just drugs. I helped my mother buy her house. I bought cars, including my baby, my lime green Corvette and my Subaru with the big "dis-stem." It was more than a sound "system," man. Chuck D said that my speakers were so big that when I opened the trunk to battle someone, the sound immediately "dissed 'em," get it? Hee,hee, har, har!

I gotta tell this story about the dis-stem right now.

Thanks to Darnell Moore—he's the reason why I got that system built. Darnell had a loud system inside of his Jeep, and I had a small speaker in my Subaru. Darnell pulled up next to me in my Subaru, opened up the trunk and we compared to see whose system was the loudest. He beat me out, man. So, I went and got an even bigger system built for my car. I came back to Darnell. I opened up my trunk and he opened his and we turned our systems up as loud as they could go. I rocked his world, Gee. Nobody else had a system louder than Flavor Flav. Darnell is no longer with us. He was shot and killed on October 8, 1990, and the system that he had in his car is still sitting at my mother's house in Roosevelt to this day. Rest in peace, Darnell.

I bought motorcycles. I took trips. I did what I wanted, and for the first time in my life, I wasn't really worried about money. I had layers of advisors to handle my career, to see to my legal issues, and to handle my taxes.

So, check this out. One night—well, first I need a sip of my Coca-Cola. This is a long story. You might find it funny, though it wasn't all that funny to me at the time.

Slurp...

Okay, so on this particular night, I've been getting high. I'm feeling good and I want to keep feeling good and I know I'm almost out of drugs. Time to make a run, naw'mean? So I hop in my 'Vette and I go. Only I'm low on cash, too, so I need to make a stop first.

It's after midnight and I'm driving the streets of Manhattan, around 93rd and Third Avenue, and I see a Citibank ATM on the corner. I get out my 'Vette and leave it running with the door open. I go to the machine. I put my card in, punch in my secret code and instead of giving me my money, the machine says "Transaction denied—Insufficient funds."

What?

I mean, I know I've got money. I know I've got plenty of money. Just yesterday when I was in the bank, there was a little less than half a million bucks in that account. There's *no way* I don't have money.

I decide that machine is just fucked up and I start looking for another one.

I see another ATM down on the next corner, so I figure I'll just walk down and give it a try.

"Insufficient Funds." Again.

I'm sure this thing is wrong, and like I said, I'm still a little high, so I walk down to the next ATM on the next corner.

"Insufficient Funds." Again.

I was furious. I knew I had money in the bank and I was convinced there was something wrong with those ATMs. I was gonna make one of them give me my damn money! So I walked from bank to bank, corner to corner, from 93rd Street all the way down to 24th Street. By then it was nearly dawn, and not one machine would spit out a single dollar for your boy, Flavor Flav. I'd walked almost all of Third Avenue from uptown to downtown, and I had no money. No money from the ATMs and no money in my pockets, not even enough for a subway token back to pick up my 'Vette on 93rd Street.

I wasn't even high any more, either. I was just mad. Furious, man.

I turned myself around and walked all the back from 24th Street up to 93rd. My car was still sitting in the middle of the street with the engine running and the door hanging open. Un-fucking-believable.

That's how I found out that my management company hadn't paid my taxes. The IRS had frozen my accounts until I paid a huge tax bill, and by the time I paid it, man, I was stone, cold broke.

I was bugging the fuck out. The only money I was making was from scattered *Public Enemy* tours. I was also selling crack and weed. I had to stop selling crack, because I was smoking it again and I was really trying not to go too deep down that path, so I was just selling weed and hydro—weed grown in water, if you didn't know. That wasn't enough to support my lifestyle or my family.

By this point, your boy, Flav, has three kids with Karren Ross, and three more with Angie Parker. I also had a drug habit that cost me thousands of dollars per day.

Having no money put me in big, big, big trouble, Gee.

What the fuck happened?

Chapter 10

The $$ of Love

FOR YOU TO UNDERSTAND ALL THIS, I gotta back up a bit so...

Rewind the tape, Gee!

Seriously, writing this book is like having a time machine, man. Hop in, turn the page and—WHAM—it's 1984. Or 1985. Around then. I get my dates a little mixed up, sometimes, naw'mean?

Here goes:

I'm in the Stevens Street Park in Freeport, Long Island. I finish selling a little crack and there's not much left, so I figure it's time to call it a day. Besides, Karren's pregnant. I'm gonna be a father for the first time soon, so the last thing I need to do is push things too far and get caught.

That's what I'm thinking when I have the feeling that I'm being watched.

I'm about to make that move out of there when cops, dozens of them, come rushing into the park, swarming like bees to a hive, man. I take off running.

I run through a hole in the fence at the back of the park and—bam. There are two Freeport Police Officers waiting for me right there at that hole in the fence.

They were ready for your boy.

Organized and shit.

They reach out to grab me, but I break to the right and I start running again. I'm little and light, and I was only about 21 or 22, so I am fast. I shake 'em, man, because I'm fast and I know the neighborhood.

As I'm running through this lady's yard, I throw the crack away.

If they catch me, I won't have anything on me and there will only be so much they can do.

I know that much from experience, naw'mean?

I turn and run through another yard, squeeze through someone's open cellar window and crouch down, waiting. I can see the police's feet as they run past the window.

I wait. I wait for what feels like a long time. It seems like hours have dragged by, man. Hours. I'm sure they must have given up the search by now. I'm sure they must have gone.

Finally, I squeeze back out the window and start running again. I turn the corner and...

There they are—six or eight cops, with guns drawn.

I throw my hands up. "Don't shoot me!" I shout. "Don't shoot."

"Get down on the ground," one officer yells.

Your boy gets down on the ground, shitting bricks, yo.

They come over, cuff my hands behind my back and the whole nine. Off we go to jail.

I expect to cool out in a holding cell for a few hours, but once I get there, they want to talk.

"So kid, where'd you get the drugs from?"

I just look at them. I don't say a word.

Let me tell you straight up, man—I've been a lot of things in my life, but one thing I have never been is a rat. I hate rats.

"Kid, we asked you a question. Where'd you get the drugs from?"

I still say nothing.

One of the cops grabs a phone book, a big, fat, yellow pages, and puts it on my head. Then the other one takes out his billy club.

"You can make this a whole lot easier on yourself if you'll just tell us—where'd you get the drugs from?"

I keep my mouth shut and just stare at them.

WHAM!

That club comes down on my head.

WHAM! The club comes down again. WHAM! WHAM! WHAM! At least eleven or twelve times. After every blow, they shout, "Where'd you get the drugs from?"

I still don't say a word.

I am not a rat. I'm not going to say nothing to take anyone else down, man. After all, no one made me go out there and sell that stuff. It was my own decision and if you're going to do something, be man enough to take your own weight. I am not a rat and I hate fucking rats.

So I don't say a word.

When they finish with me, I have the worst headache in the world. I don't think I've had a headache that bad since. They throw me in a jail cell. For a little while, that's that. Then, about five hours later, one of the guards comes by with a plain baloney and cheese sandwich, white bread, no mayo and a carton of milk.

That is the best sandwich in my life, Gee. Best milk, too. Eating that sandwich is the best feeling ever, especially after taking five hours of interrogation and being fucking starved. In jail, you learn to appreciate something as simple as a bull pen sandwich. It's the shit, folks, no lie, but that don't mean I want to return to jail to get another one.

Hee,hee, har, har!

Hell, no. I don't want to eat any more of them—but I'm glad I lived to tell you about it.

I spent twelve hours in jail that time. It was a misdemeanor because I didn't get caught with anything on me, and the amount I sold was small, so after just twelve hours,

I was on the streets again—right back to doing what I had been doing.

First, I went home to my girl, Karren Ross.

Karren was one of the first loves of my adult life, man, and for a while we had a really great relationship. I had had crushes on girls before me and her got together, but all of the other girls I'd been with had been real short term. We'd be in love for a bit, then there'd be lots of drama, then we'd break up.

Karren was my first true love, and we were together for almost ten years. When it ended, it ended bad, with lots and lots of drama, Gee.

That drama broke your boy down. It really, really did.

I met Karren and her brother Darren Ross (Flash Master D) when I was working at the Adelphi University radio station, WBAU. Karren worked at the station answering the phones.

I didn't have a girlfriend at all at the time and Karren was *fine*. She reminded me of Janet Jackson, and at that time I had a *huuuuge* crush on Janet Jackson. Karren was a real cute girl and I remember thinking to myself, "If I ever had a baby with her, she would be beautiful."

She moved in with me and my moms in 1985. She was still in high school, in her senior year, and I remember her going to school from my mother's house. She took your boy to her senior prom—yeah boyee! It was the first prom I had

ever been to. I didn't go to mine. Remember, I dropped out of
school after the tenth grade—a very big mistake that I made
with my life, and one I'm still working on correcting.

I dropped out because I was always getting in trouble,
getting high off weed and going back and forth to Nassau
County jail for selling drugs, burglaries, suspicion of rob-
bery, loitering and things like that. I'd get arrested, they'd
hold me for a day or so, then let me go. Even the drug possession charges were all misdemeanors and the penalty was a
$100 fine or a few days in jail. Most of the time, I didn't serve
even a week's worth of jail time for any of the charges, but it
happened enough that I missed a lot of school. I dropped out
at the age of 17.

I did *try* to get my diploma. I tried night school, but I
didn't last. Why? Well, you know. Your boy *does* like to hang
out, maybe a little too much. I kept getting into trouble for
one thing and another thing and another thing. It was hard
to go to school, naw'mean? Without a high school diploma, it
was hard to get any kind of decent job, so that took me back
to the same stuff I'd gone to jail for in the first place—stealing, selling drugs, snatching pocketbooks and all that. For a
while there, I was in a pocketbook snatching frenzy, me and
my boys. I regret it now, but back then, it was what I did. For
the money, man. It was what I did to survive, naw'mean?

Then Karren got pregnant and that was one of the happiest days of my life.

To know I had a child coming into the world was an exciting thing, and I wanted to be involved. I went with her to her doctor's visits, and—check this—I actually took Lamaze classes with her.

I wanted to do better, but somehow, even knowing I was going to be a father didn't stop me from using drugs. Drugs were all around me. Living in Roosevelt, I just couldn't seem to say "no" to them. My family was concerned because they saw that I was just out of control, going wild in the drug life and I couldn't seem to break free. They thought a change of environment might help me get myself straight so I could take care of Karren and the baby, too, when it came.

My cousin Rhonda came to Long island from Connecticut to get me. I was supposed to go back to Bridgeport with her get myself straightened out.

Karren was okay with that and we piled in my car one night to drive to Bridgeport for our new start. On the drive, Karren and I got into this heated argument. I mean it was seriously heated. I can't remember now what it was about, but I was driving the car at about 85 miles an hour when, next thing I know, Karren punched me in the eye! She hit me so hard I seen a big blue flash of light, man.

I slowed the car down and pulled over. I got out of the car with my eye all swollen, Gee. It was ugly. Karren was big and pregnant and she got out of the car. She was still yelling at me. My eye was swelling so bad that I could barely see out of it. I was just furious with her, man.

Mad, mad, mad.

I didn't want to hurt her, and I didn't want to hurt the baby, but I was so mad that I kicked her in the shinbone and she buckled over.

To this day I regret it, and I'm telling you, I don't care what you've read or heard about me, Flavor Flav never hit a woman unless she *made* me do it, but at that time, I wasn't giving a flying fuck. She punched me in the eye while I was driving at highway speed! She could have killed all of us, including the baby!

That wasn't cool, Gee. It wasn't cool and Karren shouldn't have done that to me while I was driving.

Bridgeport didn't work out, but Karren and I ended up making up and the whole nine. We went back to Roosevelt and everything started up all over again.

That was how it was between us—we'd get into it about something, start going at each other, make up and move on. At least that's how it went until the end, when Karren started on a new tactic. She'd pick a fight with me and when I didn't fight back, she'd keep at me more and more until I hit her. Then she'd call the cops on me and paint me as some kind of killer or something.

It was a relationship black hole, man, one that just left me hanging between violence and jail time, naw'mean?

The thing that kept us together for as long as we were was the kids, man.

I love my kids, man. Even before they were born, I was in love with them. When Karren was pregnant that first time, I was especially excited. I was there when Shanique was born.

We didn't know if we were having a boy or girl. Technology then wasn't like today. In 1986, you couldn't find out what you were having. You had to guess. At the hospital, in the delivery room, Karren was pushing and pushing and the hole of her vagina started opening and I saw something black in the middle of the hole and I thought, "That's a scalp." It opened even wider and there was the head. The doctor reached in and helped the shoulders come out, then Karren pushed the rest of our baby out.

Woooowww. Shanique was now in the building!

The baby was all gray, but she looked just like me. Shanique Yvette Drayton was born on February 6, 1986, and lemme tell you, she was me in baby form.

I was happy. I went home, got some cigars and passed them out to all the boys. We had drinks and celebrated a bit. Now, I'm a father, but I'm also starting to be a rapper and a hype man, so I wasn't home as much.

That caused us problems.

Like I said, it's 1986, right? *Public Enemy* had just signed with Def Jam and our first single "Public Enemy #1" was getting some play. We started going out on the road to do shows here and there, too. We went to Philadelphia, and at that time, Lady B was the radio jock for Power 99 in Philly. We went down to the station, did Lady B's show, and then that evening we did a concert at a club. At this club, I met a girl named Abby.

Well...

I really liked Abby and we started talking on the phone a lot. Sometimes, I would even drive down to Philly to see her, naw'mean? We were really just friends, that's all. Nothing sexual ever happened between us. She didn't have a boyfriend, but she was a very faithful girl and she was really feeling your boy, Flavor Flav. So was Karren, who was home with our baby, Shanique.

The worst mistake I could have ever made was to cheat with Abby on Karren. That bit me on the ass, really, really hard, Gee.

One night, Abby came out to Roosevelt to my mother's house, where Karren and the baby were staying. She and Karren got to talking and after that day, things were never, ever completely right with me and Karren again. That's when it all really started falling apart. I tried to get myself out of it, but folks, these girls were a little too smart for me. They nailed me to the wall like Jesus to the cross, man. They really socked it to your boy from both ends.

I ended up cutting Abby off. I wanted to try to get my girl back, man. As we were trying to get our relationship together, babies were being made. Karren got pregnant a second time about nine months after Shanique was born. We were having serious problems by then, but we stayed together through the pregnancy, and my son, William Jr., was born in 1987.

His nickname is "Man." I missed being there when Man was born. I was on my way to the hospital, but he came quick and I missed it. I was really happy because now I had a son. It was huge. WOW. Nobody could tell me nothing—I had a *son*. I guess that's how my father felt when he had me. He was a big shot back in the day, and I felt like a big shot when Man was born.

Me and Karren stayed together, but our relationship was very choppy. *Public Enemy* was taking off and there was more money coming in so I moved Karren out of my mom's and into our own place, which helped. About nine months after Man, Karren was pregnant again.

This time my daughter Karren Elizabeth Drayton was born —another very happy day for me. But the relationship with her mother? Gee, it was a mess.

Karren would do stuff to try to provoke me, so I would hit her and go to jail. She would purposely have me locked up just for spite.

The last time me and Karren got into it, it was at my mother's house in Roosevelt. My kids were at the kitchen table eating when me and Karren started arguing, and then she got really heated. She was yelling and screaming and it was upsetting the kids. They started cryin'.

I don't like for nobody to make my kids, cry, man. Nobody disrespects my mother's house, either.

"Get the fuck out of here!" I told her. I was yelling now, too. "Get out of my mother's house!"

We're out on the lawn now. Karren had really lost it by then and she got right up in my face and smacked me as hard as she could.

Man, I snapped.

I drew back my hand—and let me tell you, I was so angry it felt like I reached into my back pocket and all the way from Africa. I just smacked her right in her face.

She called the cops, and by the time they got there, her face was starting to swell. She knew what she was doing, man. That was some self-inflicted pain. I went to jail for that, and the media was all over the story.

I got charged with domestic violence and this time I stayed in jail for almost a month. It was 1991—"Apocalypse '91" was about to be released—and the whole incident made the news. *The New York Post* had a good time with that. The headline read "Rap Star Beats Lover" and the worst mistake *The New York Post* made was putting my mother's address in the paper. That's what made me write the record "Letter to the New York Post" that was on the "Apocalypse '91: The Enemy Strikes Black" album.

My group was pissed with me because a domestic violence charge put *Public Enemy* and everything we stood for in a bad light. Everybody was telling me that I was out of control and that I needed to get myself straight. I didn't want people seeing me as the kind of man who beat up on women.

I was never a woman abuser. I wouldn't be the one to initiate a fight and that's what people didn't know or understand.

Like I said, I never hit a woman who didn't make me do it to defend myself. Karren, and most of the other women in my life, had issues with anger where they would start punching and thumping on me. My girl, Angie, once beat me up, but that's another story.

Karren's hatred for me escalated. She accused me of not paying child support, and she took me to court. That made the news, too. I paid, but it wasn't like it seemed. I had been paying, taking care of her and our kids, all along. We just hadn't needed to get the courts involved until she got mad and wanted to embarrass me.

She wanted it to seem like I was a deadbeat dad, but it wasn't true, man. We were done as a couple, but I still wanted to see my kids, even though their mother was stirring up a pot of drama. No matter what was going on with Karren and me, I was always close with my kids. They were like my best friends, and everything, naw'mean?

She kept trying to take me down, but I wouldn't fall. I wouldn't stay down, no matter what. So, I guess she said to herself, "There's gotta be some way I can get at this motherfucka. Yeah, I know what it is! I'll use the kids."

She was right.

She took my kids to court and she coached my kids into saying that I'd done things to them that I never did, things that I never *would* do, Gee. Never.

None of it was true, but I lost custody of them, anyway partly because of a couple of Correctional Officers (COs) who were real assholes, and partly because of those awful allegations Karren got the kids to make against me. They didn't know what they were saying. They were little, only five, six and seven years old.

I was locked up in the Nassau County Jail when the time came for the hearing about my kids. The COs called me to go to court, and when I got down to the clothes box to take my jail clothes off and put my street clothes on, they saw who I was and started fucking with me. They kept me from going to court on purpose. I told the COs, "Look, man, I gotta get to court!" They didn't like me and they wouldn't arrange for me to attend the hearing. My not showing up before the judge at the hearing made it look like I didn't care, and like I didn't want my kids. They didn't know that I was doing everything I could to get out of jail and come to the hearing to fight for them.

I have a very strong feeling that those COs and the judge teamed up on me. It was a big conspiracy to make sure that I lost my kids.

Man, that was a blow for your boy, Flavor Flav. I'm not gonna say I'm the best father because I know I've made my mistakes, but I love my children and I always wanted to be around them. I've always done my best to take care of them. That's the truth, folks. I don't care what you've read in some newspaper or on some blog. I've always done the best I could for my kids. I've never done anything to hurt them and I never will.

This was 1992, and it just continued a serious downward spiral for me.

My losing Shanique, William and Karren made me not care about getting clean. I just didn't care anymore. I was smoking and smoking that crack. That was my escape, man, and I escaped every damn day.

In a way, I thank God for those drugs and how much I was using because when I was using, I just stayed in my house. I stayed as high as I could get, and being high kept me from doing some of the things to Karren that went through my head. I was angry at Karren, man. I was angry enough to pre-meditate lots of things. Things I thank God I didn't do, or I'd be writing this part of this book from a prison cell instead of out here on a boat on beautiful Lake Las Vegas, naw'mean?

More than that, I thank God for actually letting me *live* through all of that because there were a couple of times I wasn't sure I was going to make it. Once, I even left my body, man. Yeah, I had an out of body experience.

I smoked so much crack in my mother's basement one night—I must have smoked about $1,600 worth—that when I laid down to sleep, I felt myself rising up, out of my body. I went through the ceiling and I was in my mother's living room, and then higher and higher, through the roof of her house and up into the sky. The weird thing was, no matter how high into the sky I went, I could still see my own body, lying on that bed in the basement.

Finally, I felt something pushing me—dragging me—back down again. The rising had been really slow and pleasant, but that trip down was really fast, like some kind of roller coaster or something. I came back through the roof of my mother's house, back down through the second floor and landed back in my body with a slam.

I guess that was God letting me know He wasn't done with me yet. He had plans for me. He was giving me another chance.

Maybe He wanted me alive to teach people about the damage that drugs can do to your life. Maybe that's why He let me become an icon and have that kind of power, because when I get on the mike, I'm like E. F. Hutton, naw'mean? When E. F. Hutton speaks, people listen! That's one of my goals, now, man. To go around and talk about the dangers of drugs. If you put me in front of a crowd of 50,000, and just 10 people hear me, that's a great day in the neighborhood, folks. That's a start.

Let me tell you, people:

Drugs are easy as hell to get on, but they are hard as hell to get off! I am a witness. A living witness, thank God. Even after I had that experience of being out of my body, even after I lost my kids, even after all the jail time, it just seemed like the drugs had a hold on me. They kept calling me, and I kept answering. I couldn't say no to them. I just couldn't stop.

Chapter 11

An Icon on Lockdown

I STARTED GETTING LOCKED UP FOR drugs again. Yeah, I was "Flavor Flav," but if you think celebrity is protection, you're wrong. Man, the cops would be like, "Hey, it's Flavor Flav!" and then they'd search me, hoping to find a little marijuana or something. Motherfucking cops. It was mostly the 44th precinct cops out in the South Bronx, trying to make a name for themselves, pretending like they'd caught some big time criminal or something. Every time, they'd booked me at the station and when it was time to take me to the holding pens before going to court, they'd call the media! They done called *The New York Post*, *The Daily News*, and every other media outlet they could get, folks. They were using your boy to get higher ranks and make the news.

"Okay, Flav, the cameras are out there."

I'd put my hood up, trying to hide my face. I mean, it was embarrassing, man. It wasn't like I was trying to step out there like I was proud of myself. I wasn't proud of it at all, so I'd put my hood up. As soon as we stepped out of the station and got in front of those cameras out there, those cops would rip my hood off so the cameras could get their shot of me in handcuffs, with them just standing there beside me, smiling.

Motherfucking cops, man.

I didn't have it hard in jail most of the time. I was famous. Even the COs were fans. There were times when I did get my balls busted, but for the most part, it was like a revolving door, man, in and out of the Tombs, the jail in downtown Manhattan. There were times when word would get out that Flavor Flav was in the Tombs and it was sorta like I was the "the man" in the jail, but only a little. For the most part, I was just another inmate.

Then there was the time they say I shot at my neighbor.

I don't remember that, man. They say I did it, but if you wanna know the truth, I was too high to know what the hell I was doing, but I got locked up for it, all the same.

I was living in an apartment at Executive Towers in the Bronx by then.

I was smoking so much crack that night that I started hearing voices through the wall. I was so paranoid that I thought I heard my baby crying next door. I thought my neighbor had my family in his house. That's what drugs do. They send you out of your mind, naw'mean?

I was so convinced that my family was in this guy's house that I got my gun and I went next door. I knocked on his door, he opened it and I busted in, man.

I was like, "Yo, man, where's my family? I know they're in here."

He was like, "Hey, they ain't here."

I was sure they were there, so I was looking and looking all around his apartment. I seen him as he ran for the hallway. I chased him out into the hallway and down 23 flights of steps. By the time I got to the lobby of my building, which was crowded with people, he came toward me, making gestures like he was going to do something to me. That's when I pulled my .380 out.

I told him, "One more step and I'm going to shoot you, Gee."

He started backing away from me, right out the building. I don't remember anything other than him backing out of the building. I don't remember firing at him. All I remember after that was me going back upstairs and putting my gun away.

The police came, about 38 of them, all crowded into the lobby. They asked me to come down and I did. When I came off the elevator, every single cop drew his gun on me. There were so many guns on me, if anyone had started shooting, all those cops would have shot each other.

They took me down to the 44th precinct, again, and I did three months for aggravated assault out at Rikers Island.

My lawyer, Charles Johnson, handled my case. In the end, I beat the gun charge, but the guy still sued me for emotional distress.

Getting locked up that time cost me the opportunity of a lifetime, the chance to be in a commercial with the greatest basketball player to ever play the game—Michael Jordan.

I've met Michael a couple of times, and once I even got to play basketball with him. I met him the first time at a Nike Convention at the Colorado Springs Hotel. If that stuff hadn't happened with my neighbor, we would have done the commercial together a few months later. Can you imagine doin' a shoot with Mike?

Woowwww...

I'll never forget seeing him that first time. He had on all white—white pants, white shirt, a white hat, and white sneakers or shoes. I can't remember which. I never took gymnastics, but let me tell you, I was *flippin'* when I met Mike and everything, you know. He was just sitting there in a chair, and his legs were stretched out and I was like, "This is unbelievable, man! This is amazing!"

I met Charles Barkley and Moses Malone during that same Nike Convention! Yeah, man, we was getting it in that trip! I got to ride on the famous Nike airplane with Phil Nike and everything because Hank was doing a project with Phil's son. I got to go along for the ride.

Sometimes, it's nice to be me!

Hee, hee, har, har!

Me and Hank were sitting out poolside at the hotel, and I remember Michael Jordan saying, "Man, I've got more money than God."

Wowwww, Mike. That's a whole bunch of dough!

Hee, hee, har, har!

I had to go take my daily squirt, so I headed to the restroom. As I'm standing to do the pee-pee thing, this tall guy comes to in to use the urinal next to me. I look up at the guy. He's real tall, and I know he's a basketball player. He looks kinda familiar. So I said, "Yo, what's your name, man?"

He looked down at me and he says, "Yo man, Flav, that's fucked up. You don't know who I am?"

"No, man."

"That's fucked up. I know who you is."

"I'm bad at names and faces, man. Tell me."

The tall guy shook his head.

"No man, that's fucked up. I'm not telling you."

And that was that.

I was done doin' my thing, naw'mean, so I left the men's room and went back to Hank. A little while later, the tall guy from the men's room came out to the pool, too, and was sitting a little ways from us.

"Who's that?" I asked Hank.

"That?" Hank looked at me like I'd lost my damn mind. "That's Charles Barkley, nigga! What the fuck is wrong with you?"

Man, I almost shitted my pants. I jumped up. I practically ran over to where Charles was sitting.

"I'm so sorry," I told him. "Man, I don't know where my head is at!"

He was like, "Don't ever forget me, Flav. I don't forget you. Don't forget me!"

Trust me, if there's one basketball player I'm not gonna forget again, it's Charles Barkley.

I'm also a big fan of Moses Malone. I remember having fun with his name: "That's Moses, and don't ever leave him-mmmalone!"

Get it? I used to say that on the mike and people used to die laughing.

Once I went to the Houston Athletic Center where the Rockets were practicing. I got to meet Avery Johnson, and Moses Malone was there. Charles Barkley was playing with Houston at that time. I had the privilege of stepping out on the court and playing one on one with Moses.

That was a big deal, but not as big as when I played Michael Jordan.

Yeeeaaah boyyyeee!

The second time I met Michael Jordan was when he hosted *Saturday Night Live* and *Public Enemy* was the musical guest.

I was going crazy over Michael Jordan, because even though I'd met him once, it was still a big deal. I was star struck, and why not? He was the greatest basketball player ever. You know you'd be star struck if you met him. You know it. Who can help it?

It was a great show. Spike Lee came down to hang out with us. The Rev. Jesse Jackson was on the show, too, reading that children's book, *Green Eggs and Ham.*

Funny shit!

The third time I met Michael Jordan, I was in Chicago at a Best Western Hotel. I had a suite on the Penthouse floor, and right next to mine was another suite and Robert Kelly had it—you know him as "R Kelly." R Kelly likes to shoot hoops, too, and I remember saying to him, "Yo, R! Whenever you go play ball, I want to go, too. Take me with you, take me with you. Take me with you!"

Hee, hee, har, har!

So, one day I saw him at the hotel and he said, "I'm going now, man."

We drove down to the Chicago Athletic Center and as we were going up the stairs to the second level where the courts were, I felt someone pat me on the ass twice.

"Hey, what's up, baby?"

I turned around fast, and I'm thinking, *"Who is this patting me on the ass like this?"*

Then I said, "Oh snap! It's Mike Jordan!"

He passed me and R Kelly and went up the stairs.

The basketball courts were crowded and we had to sign up on this list just to get some time on the court. Finally, me, R Kelly and three other guys got the chance to play with Michael Jordan and his boys.

We lost the first game. I didn't even get the ball much. They were kinda hogging it, but I didn't think much of it. I was on the court with Michael Jordan! I was happy whether I got to hold the ball much or not.

We signed up for another game, and we were losing that one, too. Mike and his boys were just dominating the floor, of course. He ain't the best for nothing, naw'mean? So, I said to myself, "Hey man, you're on the court with Michael Jordan. I'm gonna get something out of this."

I called him over and I said, "Yo, Mike! Stick me, Gee! Stick me! Stick me!"

I started dribbling, trying to do some of those Meadowlark Lemon tricks. I threw up a wild-ass shot, and when the ball left my hands, I closed my eyes and started praying:

Please go in, please go in, please go in...
The ball floated closer and closer to the rim...
Next thing you know... *swish*.
Nothing but net.

The whole gym jumped up and went crazy! Michael Jordan was chasing me around the court, mumbling. It was a fun moment, one of the best moments of my life. I hit two points on Michael Jordan, at the time that he was leaving baseball and going back to basketball.

I know it was lucky shot, Mike, but it was on you and it went in. So deal with that one, Mike!

Hee, hee, har, har!

The fourth time that I saw him, which was the last time, was just a few years ago. Me, Liz and Karma were in Maui and Mike was playing golf there. I tried my best to get close enough to introduce him to my family, but they had that golf course locked down, man. We kept running around in the hot sun, trying to say "hello," sweating like dogs, and when we finally got close enough for me to yell, "Yo Mike! Yeeeah boyyeee! Flavor Flav!" He just sorta saluted us and drove off in his golf cart to his next hole.

I was like, "Ain't this a blip?"

We'd run across that golf course to say hello, but Mike couldn't give me the time of day. It kinda hurt my feelings. We went back to the front of the hotel where we were staying and rented a golf cart. I had this guy to try to drive us onto the course to catch Mike, but they wouldn't even let us on. I was told, "He's having a private game. Would you like to write him a note?"

So I did.

I told him it was Flavor Flav, and that I wanted him to sign my son's sneakers. Mike Jordan sent a note back, "I don't want you to come out now, too dangerous. I'll catch you later."

I was crushed. I just wanted him to sign the Jordans Karma was wearing and meet Liz. I wanted to see him again. He was one of my favorite people. Him not giving me the time of day hurt my feelings, man.

Who can be mad at Mike for long? Not me. Even though I ran through the heat with my baby and my girl and he dissed me, I still love him. He's the best player to ever touch a basketball. There will never be anybody better than Michael Jordan.

I hate that I missed that chance to do a commercial with him, all because they say I shot at my neighbor. I still really don't think I did, but I honestly don't know.

I was that high.

When I got out of jail on that charge, my friend, Hank Shockley, took me to the Betty Ford Center out in California. I was there for a month, trying to get myself together.

Hank took me out there because *Public Enemy* was on hiatus and they needed me to get myself straight. My drug use had reached a real high point and it was affecting everything—my relationships, my music, and my health. I knew I was at a breaking point, man, so after I got out of jail, I agreed to go to Betty Ford and try to get myself together.

Now let me tell you a little bit about rehab, folks.

I been to rehab like four or five times, and none of that shit ever worked for me.

I mean, they try and all that, and it gives you a head start because you're out of the environment where you've been getting your drugs. But as soon as you're out, as soon as you're back in your old environment, and as soon as you're back in the life you were living before rehab, man, you're back to the drugs again.

That's exactly what happened to me.

I did the rehab thing, came back home, and started getting high again.

As soon as I got back to the Bronx, I was back to marijuana and crack. I was back to selling, dealing and using. Mostly using. I was back to being in and out of jail for possession. *Public Enemy* was working on "Muse Sick N Hour Mess Age" and touring, but even after Betty Ford, I wasn't completely straight.

I missed a few gigs due to the drugs and I missed a few shows, and the group was pissed about it. They thought I should have come back from rehab 100% cured, but like I said, it just isn't like that.

Don't think I wasn't trying to clean up. Like I said, I didn't like what was happening to my life, naw'mean? I felt awful most of the time, and I knew I was failing the people around me. My group was mad at me almost all the time, and I'd lost my kids. I wanted to do better.

There was a guy named Charles Johnson who had worked as my personal security. He wanted to help me, and I knew

I needed some help. Charles would take me up to the Westchester Marriot in Westchester, New York. That's where I would go to get away from my drug-infested neighborhood, trying to stay away from drugs. Trying to stay clean.

It wasn't really working, though.

There was a guy named Eddie Bowman, who was Charles's assistant, and Bowman used to always stay with me. Bowman used to take me to the Bronx for haircuts at a barbershop called Oscars on 149th Street. One day as I was walking up 149th Street, I seen this girl walking along all pigeon-toed. She was Puerto Rican, and really cute, wearing this sexy little orange dress. I was watching her walk, thinking to myself, "I wonder what it would be like to have a Spanish girlfriend?"

Yeah, boooyyyeee!

I stopped the girl and I said to her, "What's your name?"

She said, "Angie."

Angie had a Cleopatra hairdo. They called it the "doobie" back in the day. She could have styled it any way she wanted to and she still would have been mad fine!

Hee,hee, har, har!

I had to have her. I *had* to. We exchanged numbers, kinda. I gave her my number, but she gave me the number to the pharmacy near her house. At first I thought she was dissing me, but it turned out that her family had figured out some kinda way to tap into the pharmacy line at night so they could make phone calls for free!

Hood smarts, man. Don't knock it!

I could only call her at certain times, or I'd get the pharmacist. We did talk on the phone a little bit, and one day I invited her to go up to Westchester with me. She accepted. I got to know her and we fell in love. Yes, love.

Your boy, Flavor Flav, was in love again.

After all that shit with Karren, I was hoping I could do things better, naw'mean? I wanted things to be good between us.

I used to drive my van, Corvette or my Subaru to see Angie all the time. I met her mom, and her brothers—George, Jose, Ronnie and Danny (who we called Bebo). I used to just go to see her all the time. We started dating really heavy, and one day she calls and tells me she's pregnant.

That was another happy day for me. I always wanted to know what it would be like if I had a baby with a Spanish girl, and now, folks, I was gonna get to see what my half-Spanish, half-Flavor Flav child would look like!

Hee, hee, har, har!

As much as I loved Angie, and as excited as I was to be a dad again, my drug use continued. I managed to keep it away from Angie for a good long while, but finally, she started to know something was up. I got honest with her and I let her know that I had a drug problem, a serious one. At that time, she understood and told me she still loved me anyway.

Those words were like music to your boy's ears. Everyone else in my life was giving me shit about how much I was using, but Angie just wanted to see me get some help and was gonna stand by her man, naw'mean?

Wowwww.

I used to take Angie out to Long Island and we'd stay at the Holiday Inn at Lynbrook-Rockville Center. We were there the night that Angie went into labor, because I remember putting Angie and her big stomach in my Corvette and we drove all the way out to Mt. Sinai Hospital in Queens, which was about thirty-five to forty minutes away. I think I got there in about fifteen minutes. That's where my daughter, Da'Zyna Simone Drayton, was born.

I know you folks are gonna think I'm kidding, but the day Da'Zyna was born was one of the happiest days of my life. I was happy because I was gonna get the chance to be a father again. I missed Shanique, Man and Karren so much, naw'mean? Once again, I was looking at myself in my baby's face. It was like, "Yo, that's me in light skin!" I got to see what I looked like with light skin and shit!

Hee,hee, har, har!

After the baby was born, I moved Angie out of her mother's house and into the apartment at Executive Towers.

I was making money the usual ways: with *Public Enemy*, but after 1994's "Muse Sick N Hour Mess Age," the group was on hiatus again and there really wasn't that much happening with the group on a regular basis. Occasionally, I still sold drugs, but not so much selling was happening, naw'mean? I was using waaayyy more than I was selling.

It was harder and harder to use and still take care of business, like I'd been able to do before. I'd lay off a little bit to work on the music or to do a show and not get kicked out of the group, but the drugs kept calling me.

I kept answering. Even some serious injuries couldn't keep me from using and abusing, naw'mean?

I bought myself a motorcycle.

I had never had one, but I had always been fascinated by mini-bikes. When I was young, I remember my friends and I used to break into this place that sold lawnmowers and steal the motors so we could build mini-bikes.

Now, I finally had enough money to buy one.

I got it from the Honda place in Freeport, picking out one of the fastest street bikes they made—a CBR 600. It was a beautiful machine and very colorful—all purple and pink and blue and black. A really pretty bike. Cost me about $8,500.

It was brand new when I took it out to my boy, Keith Shockley's, house in Westbury, Long Island. I was showing off, trying to get it to burn rubber without moving. I gave the bike a lot of gas, and put it in first and let the clutch go. The tires started spinning like crazy! Then I let the brake go by accident and the bike popped up on one tire, then it hit the ground.

CRASH!

I was like, "Ohhhhhh nooooo!"

It was trashed, man. That bike's plastic body was broke into pieces. There was oil and gas all over the street. I was embarrassed, and Keith, being the knucklehead he is, was just dying laughing at me. I had to call a tow truck to come and take the pieces of that bike back to Honda. They fixed it, but it cost me $4,000, nearly half what I paid for it.

If you think that kept me from riding it, you don't know your boy very well.

Once the bike was fixed, I decided to ride it from my place in the Bronx to my mother's house in Roosevelt. I had just got off the Meadowbrook Parkway and turned onto Babylon Turnpike when I saw my friend Tim Smith. Well, pretty soon Tim and I were in a race, me on that bike and Tim in his car. The speed limit was 35 miles an hour, but I hit the straight-away on that fast little bike at about 160 mph. Then I saw a big, slow dump truck coming out of the cross street about a quarter mile ahead of me. I hit the brakes hard, real hard, and I started skidding to a stop. I skidded the whole quarter mile through two intersections. I even skidded past my mother's house. If the dump truck had kept moving, even moving slow, I probably would have missed it. Just barely, but I'd have missed it. But the dump truck just stopped in the middle of the street and I had only managed to slow down enough to smash into the side of it.

I broke both my collarbones and both my arms and put a great big dent in my helmet. I'm lucky I had that helmet on because I'd have been killed instantly if I had hit my head at the spot where that dent was.

So there I am, on the ground in serious pain, man. Serious pain. The cops come, right?

The cop looks down at me on the ground and he goes, "Hey, it's Flavor Flav!" He thinks it's all so funny and shit. "Hey Flav, you got a license?"

Okay, me and a driver's license is always an issue—more on that later—but this time, I actually had one. From Virginia, but it was a license, right?

So the cop takes my license, and I'm still lying there on the ground in pain. I'm thinking, "He's gonna call for an ambulance, right? Where's the damn ambulance?"

When the cop comes back, I'm sure he's gonna say something like, "Okay Flav, we got an ambulance for you on the way."

Wrong.

He comes back with a pen and some paper, and four friends in blue.

"How about some autographs, Flav?" he says stuffing the pen into my hand.

I'm laying there on the ground with two broken collarbones, and two broken arms, and he wants autographs?

Ain't that a bitch?

Motherfucking cops.

But you know what? I did it. I scribbled some shit on paper and gave it to 'em, and by then the ambulance had finally come. It was crazy for me, folks. Just crazy.

When I got out of the hospital, I went home to my place in Executive Towers so Angie could take care of me. Only that didn't work out too good. Me and Angie got into an argument over something while I was recuperating and she started beating me up.

I don't know what happened. Angie had started out being all sympathetic and shit when I told her about my drug use. She told me she loved me anyway. She was down for your boy.

The longer we were together, the less she cared about me, man. I was laid up with two broken arms, and she's coming at me like Mike Tyson. I mean it, she was beating me up. I had both arms in slings, and Angie was just pounding on me. The only way I could defend myself was with my feet, naw'mean? I started kicking out, trying to get her off me, but it was no use. She won. Angie beat your boy up that day. She really socked it to me, which really wasn't fair because I was all broke up.

That relationship was really starting to be a fucked up mess. By then we had two kids together. Da'Zyna had a baby brother, my second son, Quanah Jonathan Drayton. He paid a big price for being born in the middle of the shit that was going on between me and his mother.

One morning, when Da'Zyna was almost three and Quanah was not quite two, they woke up early. They were hungry and they were crying. I had two broken arms and there wasn't much I could do. I really couldn't cook well with both my arms in slings.

What was Angie doing while the kids were hungry and crying?

She was sitting on the couch, listening to them cry.

I've said before, I don't like to hear my kids crying, man, so I dragged myself into the kitchen and struggled to put a frying pan on the stove, open up a pack of sausages, turn on the pilot and start cooking, all with two broken arms. I'm cooking and I'm yelling at Angie, who's just sitting on the couch in the living room, refusing to so much as lift a finger. Yelling and cooking. Cooking and yelling. Back and forth between the living room with Angie and the kitchen with the sausages.

If you're cooking sausages, they make grease, right? So when they were done, I took the sausages out of the greasy pan and that grease was still sizzling. It was still really, really hot.

"You gotta make the eggs," I told Angie. "And both the babies are wet and need to be changed."

You think she got up off her rusty dusty?

Nah, man.

Angie just sat there and did nothing. *Nothing.*

I was heated. Here I've got a couple of broken arms and I'm taking better care of our kids than she is, and she's completely whole and healthy, right? As we're there arguing, my son Quanah ran past me into the kitchen. I heard the frying pan hit the floor and then I heard my son start screaming.

I ran for the kitchen. Quanah had grabbed the pan handle off the side of the stove and turned that hot grease over on his head. The grease was cooling otherwise his burns could have been worse, but still, the stuff burnt Quanah's scalp. He'd been rocking a fly little baby Afro, but that burn was so bad that his hair was just falling off his head in steaming clumps.

We had to call the ambulance and the police came, too. They did a report on us to make sure there was no sign of child abuse. I had to tell them that he never would have gotten burnt if his mother had gotten up off her rusty dusty.

To this day, Quanah has scars on his scalp and his hair don't grow even, all because he got burnt by hot grease when he was a baby at his father's house. To this day, Angie knows deep in her heart that it was her fault, and to this day, it bothers me. Every time I see him, it reminds me of that day.

We spent nights in the Burn Unit—nights in his room that I'll never forget. It was the same year that OJ went on trial for murdering his ex-wife and Ron Goldman and got acquitted. I remember spending hours sitting by Quanah's bed and then going out into the hallway where the TV was. I remember seeing the verdict being announced when OJ was acquitted. He was so happy and I was happy, too. Any time anyone talks about that case, man, I'm right back there.

That incident put a big hole between me and Angie. I had a lot of anger at her about what had happened to Quanah, but we were still trying to make it work anyway. Quanah needed us, his mom and his dad, to stay strong so he could get better, naw'mean?

We tried, but man, I gotta tell you, it wasn't easy for your boy to stay in the relationship after that.

Angie got pregnant with Kayla while we were trying to make things work. By the time Kayla Nicole Drayton was born at Lincoln Hospital in the Bronx, it was just about over between us.

I missed her birth, too, but I remember going to the hospital, seeing her lying in the bassinet for the first time, and leaning over to pick her up.

Angie said, "Flav! Don't touch her! She just went to sleep." Angie was mad already, just because I was in the room, man. "She just wanna sleep!"

I picked her up anyway.

Hee,hee, har, har!

Well, you know me, folks. I do what I do, and that was *my* kid. I was gonna pick her up and give her a hug and a kiss and welcome her into the world anyway, and I didn't care what nobody said.

Then my old man died, and the hole the drugs were digging for me got as deep as a grave.

Chapter 12

An Icon Says Goodbye

I HAVEN'T SAID MUCH about my father or that part of my life, growing up with Moms and Pops, and my two sisters, Gail and Pam. You know I was in out of trouble and stuff and I guess part of the reason was that my old man had his share of problems, too.

My father had seven children. I'm number four. My mother had three of those children, but my father had the others in another relationship. I have a half-sister named Renee, and we're about the same age. I have a half-brother named Steven, a half-sister named Felicia, and another half-sister named Tanisha. Their last names are all Drayton. My father had a whole other family, but my mother stayed with him through all of that, through the multiple jail sentences and other stuff. She is good woman, Gee. I respect her like crazy, naw'mean?

My father shot dope.

I used to watch what it did to him, and it wasn't a good reaction. He used to be sleepy, nodding and just out of it, man. He was always getting locked up for it, too. It wasn't just him doing it, either. A lot of his friends were dope addicts. That was the thing, then, just like crack was the thing in the 1990s.

I remember when I was little, me and my friend, Gary Mosley, were playing on the roof of this building, and when we looked down over the edge we saw a bunch of guys standing in a circle with needles in their arms, and guy in the middle, tapping dope from each needle into their arms. When they looked up and saw us, we ran. When we got down on the ground, we ran across those same dope addicts we'd seen on the roof. When they saw us, they chased us. We were witnesses to illegal activity, I guess. For weeks, we were tiptoeing around the neighborhood in fear of those guys. We thought they might try to hurt us or silence us.

The other thing that was big in those days was playing "the numbers," which was the 'hood version of the lottery. My dad was a writer, and I was a runner. He would write the numbers from people who wanted to take a chance at the jackpot and I would run them up the line to where they were all collected. To this day, I love gambling and games of chance, man. I guess I got that from my pops when I was just a kid.

My father and his friends would shoot dice on the neighborhood corner, and I know I was out there with him from a really early age, maybe two or three years old.

Like father like son, he was in and out of jail, you know what I mean?

Family life was tough. I peed the bed until I was almost 12 years old. Very embarrassing folks, but very true. Your man, Flavor Flav, peed the bed, folks.

Hee, hee, har, har!

Sometimes when Mom and Dad would fight, it would get very ugly, and very violent. I think that stopped by the time I was about five, but my memory ain't that good, so don't hold me to it.

Don't start thinking my Pops was a bad guy, because he wasn't.

He wasn't that different from a lot of men in that time. Men beat up their wives then. That's what men did, and nobody did much about it, I guess. I don't remember anyone calling the cops on my pops. These days, man, don't even *think* about touching a woman. Touch a woman, and you're going to jail, naw'mean? In the court of law, a woman is always right, and she always gets the last word. Why? I don't know, but that's the way it is.

Hee, hee, har, har!

Seriously, folks, the streets were all that my father ever really knew. He didn't have too much education. I didn't finish high school, but I don't think he even got to high school at all. He had some serious street degrees though, man, naw'mean? He taught me street smarts.

One thing that I had to learn is this—it don't matter who you are or what you do in the world, you have to know something about the streets because the streets is what you have to take to get to your place of employment! You have to know the routes, man, and not every route is the best one for you.

Get me?

Seriously, my Pops tried to make sure that I knew what to do in the streets, because of what he knew about them. He didn't want me to make the same mistakes he did with drugs, alcohol and all that.

He taught me about generosity. When he hit the numbers, and there were a couple of times when he hit big, for $200,000 or $300,000, which in 1966 or 1970 was a *whole lot of money*, he'd take some of it out on the town and splurge, buying stuff for just about everyone. That's where I get my tendency to splurge from—my dad. He taught me not to be greedy. After all, God says you can't keep it unless you give some of it away.

Just don't give it *all* away—that's just stupid!

Hee, hee, har, har!

You gotta give, and you gotta give whatever you give from your heart. To be blessed, you have to give with a good heart, and that's just the truth.

My father splurged and gave, and he was sincere about it. He wanted to share with people and that was his way of doing it.

Once, I brought him out on tour with *Public Enemy*. I wanted him to see what I do. I wanted him to see who he helped make—me, naw'mean? I was proud of my life, so I took him out with me, so he could get a glimpse of what I do. He joined us for stops in Washington, DC and Baltimore.

What did my pops think?

A couple of days on the road and he was ready to come home.

"This ain't for me," he said.

Hee, hee, har,har!

Because of my dad and my brother Steven, I had opened a barbershop in Freeport on Main Street. It was called Flavor's and was run by my brother, who was good at cutting hair. I bought the place because I really wanted to give my brother a place where he could really shine—and my father, too. They needed some kind of place of employment. I wanted my father to get himself out of the street, away from alcohol and dope. My father liked to hang out in the street, but it brought him nothing but trouble, naw'mean?

That fucking barbershop. Me and Steven used to be close, and now we're not. All because of that fucking barbershop.

I'll tell that story later. I'm talking about my old man, right now, Gee.

My dad had been helping out at the barbershop and everything was goin' okay, until one night, I get a phone call from my sister, Pam.

"You better come out here. Daddy doesn't look too good, and we don't know if he's gonna make it."

I was living out in the Bronx, but I put everything down and jumped in my 'Vette. I jetted out to Long Island, straight to my mother's house, and then to the Nassau County Medical Center.

He was in the ICU.

The hospital people were all like:

"Sir, you gotta have a pass."

"You need a badge."

"You need to stop at the nurse's desk."

I wasn't trying to hear any of that. I just wanted to see my dad. I ignored all of them until I found him.

He was hooked up to a respirator and had all kinds of tubes sticking out of him, but his eyes were open. I didn't know exactly what was wrong with him, but he didn't look good to me either. I could talk to him and he could respond, so I was hoping he could bounce back.

I found out later that his liver was gone. It had stopped working because of all the years of drinking and drugs that he had done.

I stayed there two or three hours, but that was hard, real hard for your boy, to see my Pops like that. It was killing me. I had to leave, and when I did, the first thing I did was get high.

Blasted.

I couldn't take it. I was medicating myself. I was medicating myself to make me forget that my dad was probably going to die soon. As I was medicating myself, I wasn't thinking that he'd still be dying when I came down from the high. I wasn't thinking that. I was thinking, "I'm fucked up in the head seeing my dad like this and I need to feel better."

I was still a little high when I went back to the hospital the next day, and things were getting worse for him.

When I seen that, it sent me deeper into a depression. I sat with him for a while. I had just recorded some new stuff for a solo project I was working on for Def Jam. I had a new Walkman and headphones, and I had been listening to it myself, trying to fine-tune it a bit. Sitting there with my Pops in the ICU, I rewound the tape to the beginning and put my headphones on my dad's ears.

I pressed "play." He listened. I watched his face, but I couldn't see any reaction. I think he liked it.

I know he did.

I took the headphones off and stayed for another hour. It was probably about 10:30 p.m. when I finally went home.

Well, I didn't go straight home.

I picked up some stuff on the way home, and once I got there, I got so high I was out of my mind. Around 1 a.m., something starting talking to me. It said, "Go to the hospital, your father needs to see you right now."

I was so high, I wasn't sure what I was hearing. I was so high, I knew that I looked high.

"Go to the hospital, your father needs to see you right now."

That voice was so sure of itself that I got up. I felt like it was God telling me to get over to that hospital right *now*, so I did it.

I was sooo high.

I managed to drive out to the hospital and get to my father's room. His respirator was still going, and his eyes were closed. I stayed there, looking at him for about 45 minutes, and then I shook him.

"Yo, Dad. Yo, Dad!"

He opened his eyes and looked at me.

"You alright?"

He nodded and closed them again.

I left, went home and got higher.

I laid down and went to sleep. Next thing I know, my mom was standing over me. She said to me, "Well, Ricco, that's it."

Automatically, I knew what that meant. I had just seen him a couple of hours before, but I was still so high, I couldn't even break down. Funerals and death—I always have a certain strength about those kinds of losses, man. It's a kind of strength that I got from him. He was always the strongest one in the room. Even when his own mother passed away, he acted like it didn't even touch him. He acted like, "Ain't nothing," naw'mean? That's where I learned about strength.

I had help. I was so high, I *couldn't* cry. I was so high, I *couldn't* break down.

I really didn't want to go to the wake or the funeral after it. I really wasn't about seeing my father's body laid out like that, but I didn't have much choice about it.

I went up to the casket and I saw him there. I just said, "Thanks, Dad" and went back and sat down with the rest of the family. Wasn't no hollering, screaming, crying and stuff, at least not then. It was that last look, just before they closed the coffin. That last look—it's the one that gets you, folks!

It got me.

Man, your boy, Flavor Flav, *lost* it. It took that whole church to pull me away from the coffin, naw'mean? I really knew then it was the last time. It was the last time I was ever gonna see the greatest man on earth—because he created one of the greatest men on earth—me, Flavor Flav.

After the funeral, I went back to Freeport, talked to my drug guys, and picked up a little something. As I'm standing on the corner talking, bird shit fell on my shoulder. Then I said to myself, "Wow, that's my dad. He's still with me."

Yeah, I know...bird shit, but they say it's lucky. Sometimes even shit can be a good thing, naw'mean?

You see, nothing is promised to us. The only promise in life that we do have is death. While we're living, let's get everything out of life that we can, while we can. Let's have all the fun that we can, while we can. When you die, you're nothing but a memory, and you want that memory to be a good one to those you leave behind.

That's one of the reasons I'm writing this book. I have a lot of good memories to share, and I'm a walking miracle, too. I coulda been dead a long time ago, naw'mean? I'm still here, and I guess that means God still has a plan for your boy.

Yes, my father's death did send me deeper into the path of drugs. When he died, over half of me went with him.

Chapter 13

Grieving at the Phoenix House

M Y FATHER'S DEAD AND in the ground, man and I've left Freeport for home, in the Bronx.

I'm around the corner from my apartment and I've just bought a little something for the evening.

Drugs, of course.

I'm walking home, minding my business, when a police car pulls up behind me and two officers jump out.

"What?" I ask. I mean, I ain't doin' nothing but walking. I'm about to go into my apartment building. I know they didn't see me buying drugs. There wasn't anybody back there, but here they come at me, shoving me against the side of the car and patting me down, for no damn reason.

Motherfucking cops.

Of course, they find the drugs in my pocket, and it's back to jail again for your boy, Flavor Flav.

This time, three months in Rikers Island, C-73. After I got out, I was put on probation and part of my probation was to go to rehab at Phoenix House.

My probation officer was a guy named Mr. Utel Ricketts. He really tried to help me, but like I said, until I was ready, no one really could reach me. I appreciated what he was trying to do, but the time wasn't quite right for your boy to get with the program. Phoenix House was an okay place, too. It was there that I first met a woman named Michelle, who I came to hate. That bitch worked at Phoenix House and then became a probation officer. That bitch set your boy up so that I lost my house and almost everything that was in it.

I hate that bitch so much to this motherfucking day that I'd love to tell you her full name and ruin her life.

Lawyers and people like that tell me that's a bad idea, so I won't do it, but I'd like to. I'd like to hurt that bitch's life like she hurt mine, naw'mean?

She's what I remember most about Phoenix House. I also remember that while I was at Phoenix House, I saw my boy Biggie Smalls for the last time.

I was living in Phoenix House when he and his crew stopped at a delicatessen on the corner near the rehab center. Word got around that he was there. I wasn't supposed to leave, but rules like that never stopped me from doing something I wanted to do, so I left anyway. I walked down the block, said "Whassup?" to him and then I went back to the Phoenix House.

A few months later, I got the news that Biggie got shot in LA and was dead. That took big, big, chunk out of me, naw'mean?

Biggie and I went back a minute or two.

The first time that I met him was at the LaMontrose Hotel in LA. Biggie and Lil Cease and the rest of the Junior M.A. F. I. A. were playing "Cee-Lo" with three dice. I seen the dice— like I said, I been playing dice since I was about three years old—so I walked up to them and said "Whassup?"

I didn't know who he was. It was before he was big—in maybe 1992 or 1993, I guess. Maybe later. You know your boy, Flavor Flav, don't really remember dates.

I do remember that I ran back to my room, got $400, came back and started shooting.

Man, I took all their money, their per diems, everything. I broke them. I broke them, and when I cut out, the only thing I left them with was the dice.

Yeaaahhhh, boyeee! They remember *that*.

The next morning they went up on the roof of that hotel and shot a video called "Juicy." I bet you know that one. After that, they just blew up, man.

I'm just proud to say that I took their money.

Hee,hee, har, har!

I had to tell that one... wowwww...

After I snuck out the Phoenix House to go say "whassup" to Biggie, I went back, finished my program and then went back home to try to get myself together.

Maybe I would have succeeded that time, if it hadn't been for Def Jam.

Chapter 14

Insufficient Fun

W E'RE BACK TO THE STORY I TOLD you at the beginning.

Your boy, Flavor Flav, is walking the streets of Manhattan in the wee hours of the morning, going from one ATM to another, trying to get some money.

Nothing. Not a dime.

I had to walk all the way back to my 'Vette, still parked on 93rd Street with the door hanging open and the engine running, and drive home.

I couldn't get any money from anywhere.

No one had anything to give me to hold me over. I'd been giving my family money, but they didn't have any left over to give back. Not even my brother, Steven, even though I'd invested $45,000 in that barbershop in Freeport. I bought the walls, the floors, the barber chairs, the clippers, the mirrors and even donated the clocks he put all over the walls. We called it Flavor's, and it had pictures of me inside, too.

I said, "Here bro, take this shop. Run it. Be successful."

The business wasn't doing good because my brother was the only one working there. He'd had good barbers—a ton of them—come through the shop. As soon as my brother realized they were better than he was, he would fire them!

Hee,hee, har, har!

He was alone, trying to do everything himself and not making enough money to reimburse me for all the money I put in. He mismanaged that place, and that separated us. We don't speak to this day.

Ultimately, my brother got so frustrated that he walked away from the shop altogether. He gave it to this guy we called "Little George" Ward. George still has it and its new name is Port Knox. It's still on Main Street.

I got $3,000 of my money back out of that shop. The rest is history, folks, and so are me and my brother, which is a shame because I love my brother and I miss our relationship. If he ever really needed me, I'd be right there for him.

I don't know how I got to this story, folks, but I'm telling you, family and money can lead to some real bad blood.

When I needed some help from family, there just wasn't anything coming back to me, naw'mean?

I asked my friends, but when you're asking for money, you don't have any friends, naw'mean?

Nothing. I didn't go to Chuck D or any of the guys from the group. I couldn't, man, because I had my pride. I did have one source that I figured could solve my problems.

My record label.

Public Enemy was working on a new album for Def Jam. I had a solo contract with them and I had been working on an album of my own.

I couldn't get any money because the IRS has frozen my assets. It was totally right for me to go to my record label for financial help. Artists get advances from their labels all the time, right?

Boy, was I *wrong*. I was wrong, Gee! I was sooo wrong!

Lyor Cohen was now President of Def Jam. Russell Simmons was still there, but he had less to do with the day-to-day activities of the label, so if you had a problem, Lyor was the one to see. I went into his office and I told him straight up, "Lyor, I need some money." I told him about my tax problem. I told him about Angie and about Da'Zyna, Quanah and Kayla. "My kids need diapers, milk, and all that shit. I need some money to live on, man."

Lyor just looked at me.

"No," he said. "I cannot help you at this time."

I couldn't understand why. I thought Lyor was my friend. I couldn't believe it. Here I am, signed to Def Jam as a solo artist and with *Public Enemy,* and I can't get a dime? What the fuck was going on?

Lyor started explaining that the label wasn't going to advance me a dime until they got more work out of *Public Enemy.* About how they were advancing all this money for the new *Public Enemy* album and there wasn't any more coming until it came out and they saw how it did, financially. Until that happened, there wasn't going to be any more cash for your boy, Flavor Flav, solo album or not. He didn't give a shit about me or my kids. He just wasn't going to give up the money.

I'm guessing how I looked then didn't help. I'd been using crack for over ten years, and by then I was starting to look like a crackhead, naw'mean?

I probably looked like if you'd given me a nickel, I'd have found a way to smoke it.

I couldn't take no for answer. I didn't have any money on me at all. I had relied on going to the bank or the ATM and getting some more. With my accounts frozen, I was flat broke. When your boy says "flat broke," I mean it. I didn't have anything.

I went back again a couple of days later and asked again, and Lyor said "no" again.

I was furious, man. I was so furious that they asked me to leave.

I left Def Jam's headquarters in Manhattan, and went down the street. There was this little pizza place and I went in there. I was just talking to anyone who would listen —that's how mad I was.

There was this guy there and it turned out he was a big fan of Flavor Flav. I was telling him what had happened with the label and how I was broke and my label didn't care. I didn't know him from a can of paint, man, but you know what? That guy reached into his pocket and handed your boy $125.

I've never asked a fan for anything, man. I'm not that kind of celeb. I don't get down like that, but I took it, and I was so thankful to the guy, too, because I really was broke. I didn't have the money to buy a crippled crab a crutch, man!

You know what I did then?

I took that guy upstairs to Def Jam's headquarters, right into the office where the group, *Onyx*, was sitting with Lyor Cohen. You remember *Onyx*, right? They had that song "Slam" that was huge hit in 1993, and the members have been in movies like "Clockers" and on TV on "The Shield" and "The Wire." They were in Def Jam's office that day getting ready to do an interview with a magazine.

So I burst in on that meeting and I said:

"Here's a guy from out on the street that I don't even *know*, right? I asked *him* for some money to feed my kids and he gave it to me! I asked my own record label for money to feed my family and they turned their back on me!"

Lyor Cohen turned to me all calm and cold and said in his funny accent, "It must be a tragedy."

I'll never forget that. The way he said it, and the way he looked when he said it. Cold as ice, man. That's why on *Public Enemy's* next album, "He Got Game," on the song "Shake Your Booty" you'll hear me say "Fuck Lyor."

It gets worse. He also said that until they got some more new work out of *Public Enemy*, the label wasn't releasing my solo album at all. Ever.

They didn't.

So, if they weren't going to release my solo album, then I wasn't gonna be making any money off it. If I wasn't gonna be making them any money, they weren't going to advance me any money, naw'mean?

That really damaged me. If they had put my solo project out at that time, I would have been triple or quadruple platinum. I might have sold 6 million copies, Gee. Hell, you never know what might have happened. They fucked me up to this day because they didn't put out the album at a time when I was commercially viable, man. I feel in my heart that it would have sold, man. I would have made millions. That money would have made it easier for me to have moved away from the people I was hanging with and the influence of the 'hood, naw'mean? I would have gotten myself into a nice area away from drugs, and I would have made more music, more albums.

They didn't put the album out and they fucked me up. No album meant no cash, and I ended up living in an environment that kept me around drugs. Being around drugs made it hard for me to quit using them, so I didn't quit for years and years.

Signing with Def Jam as a solo artist turned out to be one of the worst mistakes I could have made. They never did release my album, man. Never.

That's why on "Shake Your Booty," I was saying "Fuck Def Jam!" and "Fuck Lyor!" I feel like Lyor had said,"*Fuck you, Flav.*" It was shocking to me that he behaved that way, because we had always been friends. I mean real friends, man. Lyor had even tried to get me to go to meetings with him—he'd had a drug problem himself. If I had gone to meetings with that man, maybe now I'd be as rich as him!

Hee,hee, har, har!

I didn't. I stayed mad, drugged up and fucked up.

I did feel kinda funny about saying that on the song because Lyor had always been my friend, and had always wanted the best for me. At that time, I really felt like he turned his back on me.

Here's where it gets really crazy, folks.

I really feel that Lyor Cohen *not* giving me that money probably helped save my life.

I was on drugs pretty heavy then. I did need money for my family and I did need to pay my rent, but I think Lyor knew that if he had given me the money, I might have killed myself with drugs. If that was what was on Lyor's mind, then I guess I have to say, "Thank you, Lyor."

It still felt like a cold-hearted situation. He could have given me enough for diapers and milk, naw'mean?

Now, my feelings are mixed, man. On the one hand, I'm grateful now, because I'm alive. On the other hand, I'm still mad because he left me hanging and because that solo album should have been released back then!

That's when I fell out with Def Jam, and got off their label as a solo artist. To this day, there's some bad feelings there. When we tour and we do the record, "Rebel without a Pause," I say, "Fuck Def Jam" because of the way they did me as a solo artist. It's personal. My beef doesn't have to be everyone else's. I still feel that they fucked me over.

When we did the Hip Hop Honors for Def Jam in 2009, at first I refused to perform. I was feeling like, *"Why should I make them look good, when they treated me so bad?"* In the end, I thought about all the good times. I did have good times with Russell and Lyor.

I went to Lyor's wedding, man. In the Dominican Republic. He married this model named KT and it was real nice. That's where I learned to ride a motorcycle, at his wedding. The first time I got on the motorcycle and put it in gear, I drove it up a wall. My first motorcycle accident, folks—at Lyor Cohen's wedding reception, but that's another story. I also pushed KT into the pool and she chipped her tooth. One thing I can tell you is, do NOT chip a model's tooth. She was mad at your boy! Wooowww....

Still, it was good times.

Now, Def Jam has become one of the positive and power-ful entities for music and artists today.

I don't know what turned Lyor against me, but something did, and when he heard that "Fuck Lyor" on that record, I remember he said, "Take it out or we won't put the album out." I told Chuck and Hank I didn't care. I was like, "Put it out there."

Yeah, the guy left me hanging.

Left.

Me.

Hanging.

I got mad love and respect for Lyor today. I'm proud of the position he is in right now—he worked hard for it. I've seen where he came from. He's worked himself up to where he is today. He owns an empire. I'm proud of you, bro.

I'm just a few footsteps behind you now.

Back then, I was out of control, man. Rehab couldn't reach me, and my family couldn't reach me. Nothing could reach me. Then, I got a once in a lifetime opportunity that I hoped would change things for me.

Chapter 15

Chief Flavor

"**A**re you Flavor Flav?"

I hear that question all the time, folks, but this time, I heard it in an unexpected place.

Aburi, Ghana.

"I want to take you to meet my chief!"

In December 1997, a religious group organized a trip to 50 nations in Africa and the Middle East. Over 400 African Americans of all religions participated. It was the first time so many African Americans had returned, all at once, since being stolen from Africa.

Your boy, Flavor Flav, was one of them for part of the tour. *Public Enemy* participated and we were joined by several people, including Jermaine Jackson and Isaac Hayes in Ghana. We met the man who was president of Ghana then, Jerry John "JJ" Rawlings. One of the most historical pictures ever taken hung in his office—the members of *Public Enemy*, Isaac Hayes, Jermaine Jackson, Gary Byrd, Marcus Garvey, Jr. and a few others.

Jermaine Jackson and I have been friends for a while. He actually took me to my first black rodeo. I never knew there were black cowboys until we did that. I was lovin' seeing them wearing all that cowboy stuff and throwing lassoes and riding those big steers.

Woowwww....

That was amazing stuff.

Jermaine even introduced me to his mother, Katherine Jackson. When I was in Los Angeles, I used to go over there and talk to Mother Jackson, and her good friend, Ms. Louise, who became like an auntie to me.

They loved me, man, and I loved them, too. That's one of the reasons that, when Michael Jackson passed, I was the first celeb to arrive at Mother Jackson's gate. You probably saw that clip on TV somewhere, but what you didn't know is that I'm friends with Mother Jackson. I had been over to the house before, and Jermaine and I go way back.

I even met Michael Jackson himself, years before, at a party given by then-Sony Music chief, Tommy Mottola.

Michael Jackson.

What can I say, folks? It was very, very huge to my life the day I met Michael. I was standing next to one of my childhood idols, man. When I was growing up, *The Jackson 5* was the leading black group of that time. Now, I had already had the pleasure of meeting Jermaine and Katherine Jackson, but I was so star-struck that I never got to tell Michael that I knew his mother and brother. I did get to shake his hand and take a picture with him, but that was it.

That was 1988 or 1989—like I said, years ago. I'll never forget it, man. Never, as long as I live.

So fast forward with me for a second to June 25, 2009. I was in a meeting with my lawyer, Wayne Kazan, and my manager, Greg—oh yeah, I gotta tell you about Greg!—when Wayne's secretary came up to the window, and put a note up that said, "Michael Jackson has just passed away."

When I saw that note, my whole body went numb. I couldn't feel nothing. I was in such shock. I couldn't believe it. I didn't think it was true.

I wanted to get to Katharine Jackson right then. I left Wayne's as soon as I could and drove right up to the Jackson home, right to Mother Jackson's gate. It was less than an hour after the news came. When I got there, Miz Katherine and the rest of the family had just left. I'd missed them by minutes.

Even though I only met him once, losing Michael, wow. That was one of the biggest holes my heart ever had. It just broke me down. I went and sat in my car privately and I cried like a baby. Michael Jackson? Dead? No way. Come on, man. "Stop the Love you Save," "ABC," "Mama's Pearl," "Dancing Machine," "Billie Jean," "I Wanna Rock With You," "Off the Wall," "Dirty Diana," "Man in the Mirror," "Thriller," "Beat It"...

I couldn't believe the man behind all those records was dead. It didn't seem like it could be real.

I drove home that night, and stayed there. The next day I went back to the Jackson house and walked up to the gate. There was a security guard outside and he told me the family was having a private meeting.

It was a lie, man.

I know it. He just didn't want me to go in. He didn't know how close I was to Mother or to Jermaine and his family.

Being turned away like that, well, it really broke my heart. I just wanted to say to Mother Jackson, "Michael's not dead. His body is just a shell. He'll always be here. We can't see him, but now he's your Guardian Angel—and I don't mean the group that runs around the neighborhoods protecting people either. I mean the ones in our lives who've passed away. The ones we loved the most, who're now watching over us."

Who are we to question why God does what He does and everything He does? He does it all for a purpose. God must have needed an extra angel that day, so He took Michael Jackson to work for Him.

Sorry—I just had to tell that story. Talking about Jermaine got me thinking about his family and then about Michael.

I'm way ahead of myself. Your boy, Flavor Flav, has had such a life! So many memories! So many people!

Anyway, back at the ranch, I was tellin' you about Africa and traveling with Jermaine Jackson and the others, right? I told you that Marcus Garvey, Jr. was there, too, which was large for me because of what his father stood for. I learned about Marcus Garvey at the Afro American Experience at Hofstra University when I was in my late teens. That's also where I first learned to play African drums (congas.)

When the tour left Ghana for the next country, I stayed. Somehow I ended up in a town in the mountains called Aburi. The big industry there is making wooden African masks that are sold all over the world. There's a place there called the Aburi Gardens, and I was in the gift shop looking around, and that's when this kid comes up to me and says, "Let me take you to my Chief. He would love to meet you!"

His name was Ofari and we walked through the village to this house that they call "the palace." I met the Chief of the village, Nana Jing Quasi. Ofari translated our conversation.

Well, the Chief fell in love with your boy and made me his personal advisor!

There was a ceremony as I was installed as a Chief. They gave me three acres of land and a new name—Nana Quabna Abobi. That means "I am Ancobia Henny to Omar Henny."

Omar is the Chief, ancobia means "assistant," so it means I am the Chief's personal assistant.

When I go to Aburi, they serve me. If I get something myself, I am breaking the tradition. It's an amazing thing, to get the chance to go to Africa, be welcomed, become a Chief and get land and a "real" name, naw'mean? It was like, wowwww...

I grew up Methodist, attending Bethel AME Church that was right across the street from my house. I used to go to Sunday school there, and I sang my first song there when I was just five years old. The name of the song was "Jesus Be a Fence Around Me," and I still remember the words to this very day.

I sang that song and it was my greatest day in life. I was a bright, shining star on that Sunday, like I was most Sundays when I was a little kid. I loved singing and performing for the church. By the time I reached 12, church was fading out of my life in some ways. I still played bass guitar for Second Baptist Church and Reverend E. Mitchell Mellett on Merrick Road in Freeport, though.

By then, my sister had a boyfriend named Ronald Lincoln, and when he came home from jail, he was a Muslim. It was the first time I really heard a lot about the Nation of Islam, and I was curious about it. I started going to Temple 7B in Corona, Queens.

I was probably about 15 when I got hip to the Five Percenter philosophy and became a Five Percenter. A Five Percent

Muslim is an off-shoot of the Black Muslims who comes into his knowledge directly from God Almighty, naw'mean? A Five Percenter believes that the Black man is God and that only about 5% of the population has any true knowledge of themselves or their real nature. It was started by one of Malcolm X's disciples, Clarence 13X. The language of Five Percenters is in a lot of rap lyrics. A lot of rappers believe in it and that's why they call they say things about "dropping science" and shit. That's Five Percenter talk. It's also popular in the prison culture, man. I stayed a Five Percenter for 4 or 5 years, and then I ended up going back to Christianity.

Flavor Flav believes in God, man. I *believe*, naw'mean?

I still believe there's just one guy up there. Just one. These days, I call him Jesus Christ, but you can call it whatever you want, man. It's still the same.

What God revealed to me is that there are a bunch of religions. Buddhism, Christianity, Islam, Hinduism, Wicca —all of 'em worship differently and use a different name for God. At the end of the day, there's only one God who made this whole Universe. There's only one, folks. Call it want you want.

In 1994 or 95, I can't remember for sure, I went to Israel to visit my friend Desi Barmore from Freeport who was playing basketball for an Israeli team, called Bnei Herziliya. I also went to Jerusalem and walked down the road where Jesus carried his cross to crucifixion. I bought holy oils and holy water. I ate hummus with people on that road. I donated a pair of glasses and a hat to the Hard Rock café in Tel Aviv. I wanted to go back there. I felt like I was supposed to go back and talk to the people, but I never did. Maybe someday. I felt an extra sense of power when I left that place. I felt that God had got into me. I felt God telling me that I got work to do. I got work, naw'mean?

And it must be true, because I'm still alive!

Hee,hee, har, har!

Seriously though folks, there was a tourist bus bombing right after I left Israel. I feel like I got lucky for not being there then, and for surviving every other hole I've slipped into in my life.

God's got plans for your boy, naw'mean?

That's why I pray. I say thanks to Him every day that I open my eyes. Every moment that we live, God controls the moment. The only things that God lets us control are our personal actions. At the end of the day, that's how He judges us, and no one else has the right to judge us. No one. When you lay down and go to sleep, you lay down with your own shit. No one else's.

I'm telling you something deep here, man.

When I was in my mother's womb, God knew that you'd be reading this book. He knew we'd be connected like this, naw'mean? He controls the moment for us to connect here. God controls *all* the moments. We are the chosen ones because He chose us to wake up today. There are a lot of people who didn't wake up today. I tell my children, every day you wake up and you open your eyes, you gotta thank God for that. Every time you get food, you thank God for that food. There are a lot of people who are not as fortunate as you are, and the moment you start taking things for granted, God will take everything from you.

Always be appreciative to God and to everyone else in the world, too.

The devil's job is to tempt you, and to try to get you to walk away from all the good in your life. I'm at a point now where I'm just not interested in the devil's temptations anymore. Hey lady, you might have the biggest titties in the world and the biggest ass, and I might think you look great, but I'm not going to risk what I have at home for your ass and titties. Not for anything in the world. I've been there. I've been in a place where I could have any woman, lots of women, but I'm not interested in going back there. I'm not throwing away my blessings, man. I'm not throwing away the peace and love that I have at home for big ol' tits and a big ass.

All the women I've had in my life, it's amazing I didn't catch AIDS. I didn't and I'm thankful for that. Anything He created, He could destroy, too. I'm glad to have the common sense to understand that the devil is just doing his job, which is trying to steal your life if he can. God is the power, naw'mean? God is the power, and I know that. I've always known it. Most of the things I know, I feel like God taught them to me. Yes, I've heard the same words coming from preachers, too, but that's more confirming what you know in your own heart. It's just confirming what God taught me Himself. God is the only teacher I need—God and experience. Together they've made me stronger than temptation and stronger than the devil, or at least any devil with big titties and a big old ass.

Hee,hee, har, har!

It took me a while to learn that, though. The hardest devil for me didn't have titties. It was drugs.

I got home from Africa and went back to my drug-infested environment. All that powerful connection to homeland and history, man, it was lost to me.

All the spiritual connection...gone, in a puff smoke.

All the sobriety talk of rehab, over.

I got high again.

And again.

And again.

Chapter 16

The Flavor
of Rock Bottom

ANGIE AND I WERE THROUGH.

My solo album wasn't ever going to come out.

The IRS had seized my money and I was broke.

All I had to live on was the scattered money from *Public Enemy* concerts, royalties and what I made selling drugs.

I was in and out of jail, in and out of jail, in and out of jail.

It looked like the bottom for your boy, but I guess I had a little further to fall. It was like I had dived into that manhole under the 59ᵗʰ Street bridge again, naw'mean?

Most people, when they realized it was a ladder going nowhere, nowhere but 180 foot drop right into the water, well, they would have climbed back up. Not me. I had to climb all the way down so that my feet were dangling and my arms were the only things holding me up.

Drugs were like that hole, man. It wasn't enough to know that I was losing everything that I cared about. I had to find the very bottom, naw'mean?

It seemed like I kept climbing lower and lower. It was beginning to look like there wasn't a bottom, except death.

I couldn't seem to turn it around. I couldn't find a way to quit using.

I couldn't find a way to really move on and leave the Bronx and Long Island and my old environment.

I moved Angie downtown into another apartment on 3rd Avenue between 35th and 36th Streets. There was D'Agostino's supermarket across the street. I still had my place up in the Bronx but my life in the Bronx was starting to fall apart. My 'Vette and my van both got stolen from the parking garage because the garage was sold while I was locked up. By the time I got out, my cars were gone. The new owners swore they'd never had them. The old owners had taken them, so now I was riding a bike to get around. The cops were following me like they smelled bacon or something.

Those 44th precinct cops liked to stop people and search them for nothing and they kept doing it. They kept stopping me, even when I wasn't doing anything and they didn't have any real reason. They stopped me and, of course, they'd find crack on me. Never a lot—like I said, I never held a lot, but for years, I was in and out of Rikers Island for drugs and gun possession.

Yeah, gun possession.

Your boy always had a gun on him, either the .380 or a 9mm. Always. I felt like I needed it for protection because the neighborhood I was living in was so rough.

There was a time when I was riding my bike in the rain to my friend Eli's house and I had a 1/4 pound of weed stuffed in the waistband of my pants. It was about 12:30 or 12:45 in the morning, raining and freezing cold. As I was riding along, I saw the police ride pass on the other side of the street. I saw them slow down, flip a U-turn and I knew they were coming for me, even before they hit their lights.

Damn. Not again.

So they searched me and they found the weed.

"Hey Flavor, you selling weed now?" they said.

I told them I wasn't selling anything. I was going to smoke it with a friend.

"We gonna smoke today, huh?" they said. "What's this? You got a gun now, huh?"

"You know I need some kind of protection, out here by myself," I told them.

One of those cops pointed my own gun at my head and cocked it back. I was very afraid it was gonna go off, Gee. Seriously. I thank God that it didn't, but I got another visit to Rikers for that one.

About the only good thing going in my life then was my girlfriend, Beverly Johnson.

I met her in 1998, after Angie and I split up.

I had started going back and forth between the Bronx and Houston, Texas. My boy, "Black Cat" Clyde Bazil, and his wife, Gina, were trying to help me get myself straight and start my life over. He thought I needed to get out of the Bronx and I thought he was probably right, so I started heading out to Houston, trying to get myself drug-free. Black Cat wasn't the only one. My boy, Casper, in Chicago wanted me to come out *there* and see what I could do. I was between Houston and Chicago, putting together a solo album. When I went to Chicago, Casper would take me to the studio and I would record with my boy, Derrick Blocker.

I stayed with Black Cat and his family on and off for about 2 or 3 years in Houston, and the same with Casper in Chicago.

I appreciated the help, but it never really worked out, simply because something would always happen to send me back to the Bronx. As soon as I was back in that environment, I just couldn't resist, man. The drugs had a bigger hold on me than anything else in my life. I might be good for a few weeks or months out on the road with *PE* or in Houston or Chicago or wherever, but as soon as I got home, I'd forget all the promises I'd made to myself and all the progress I'd made and that would be that.

One of those times when I was back in the Bronx, I was at the Chase Manhattan Bank on the corner of Gerard and

161st Street, and I seen this short, short girl. Like 4'11", man. Really short.

"Hello," I said.

"Hello," she said.

We talked a bit while we waited for our turn for the cash machine.

I was leaving on my bike, and she had her daughter in the car and we exchanged numbers. That was how I met Bev— Beverly Johnson and her little daughter, Jasmine.

I went back to Houston, but I stayed in contact with Bev. When I returned to New York, we started dating. I invited her to my place in Executive Towers, and she spent some nights with me. I fell in love with this girl. Really, really. She was a good person. A sweet person who was sweet to your boy. She was the girl who said:

"Hey listen, boo, if you ever need a place to stay, you can come to me. And even if we break up, you can stay with me. If you need the bed, I'll take the couch—or whatever. We'll work it out. I would never, ever, ever, kick you out."

Woowww...

We stayed together for about 4 or 5 years—before she kicked me out.

Hee, hee, har, har!

Bev would visit me in the Tombs and at Rikers when I got locked up. She held it down for your boy, bringing me property and putting money on my books.

Jail was getting too familiar, man.

I was a favorite at the Tombs and at Rikers. All of the COs wanted me to work in their department. I had about eight jobs—in the clothes box, where they take your regular street clothes and give you jail clothes; in the mess hall, cooking; in the barbershop; with the SPA- the suicide prevention watch- for the bug out people. I had a job outside in the Rec Yard. I got to see everyone in the joint, naw'mean? I even ran across my boy, Chi Ali, on his way up to Sing-Sing when he was convicted of murder in 2001.

I was locked up with all kinds of people—people who committed murder, con artists, rapists, and arsonists. For the most part, I was just another inmate. I didn't try to get special treatment because I was celeb or nothing. Protective custody is for suckers. I'm a *man,* so I went GP— general population—and I'm thankful for the guys who had my back in jail when things got rough, which they sometimes did. The COs, too. Most of the time, I could walk around without a pass, which technically isn't allowed. I made some friends, and got to do a lot of interesting jobs because the COs were fans.

I had some bad times, too. I even spent some time in "the hole," solitary confinement, for fighting. Yeah, your boy was fighting. People would accuse me of stealing their stuff, personal items and other properties. I'd deny it, though sometimes...

Well, you know. Stealing was a part of my world then.

Once after my friend Casper, his wife Pam, and my girl
Bev visited me, three COs jumped me as I was headed back to
my cell. They were punching me and stomping me and I was
screaming "Help! Help!"

No one came.

No one comes between the police and a beat down. That's
rule number one, naw'mean?

I never knew why they were beating me up. I mean, three
big policemen are beating me up and I don't weigh more than
coke bottle? Man, they fucked me up. They hid me until the
bruises healed. They didn't want me out in the general population like that.

I actually did a radio show for New York's HOT 97 from
jail. It was called "Flavor Flav's Home Jams." My engineer
was Dennis Riviera and that's what I did—play people's jams
from home. I'm the only one who ever did a radio show from
jail, Gee.

Another time we did this stunt where I stayed on the radio
for 24 hours straight, pretending that I had hijacked the station and wouldn't let it go until my demands were met. That
was some funny shit, man. We had everyone thinking I had
taken the radio station hostage. HOT 97 should give me my
own award one day. I did stuff on that station that no one
had ever done, and no one will ever do.

I spent two and a half more years in and out of jail for driving violations and drugs. This was between 2000 and 2002.

I was in jail when I heard that my boy Jam Master J had been shot and killed.

I was on Riker's Island in the C-76 building on the night he got shot, serving a mandatory one year sentence. I was in my dorm. A bunch of guys were in the Rec Room where the news was on TV. I remember clearly everybody yelling and calling me.

"Yo, Flav! Something happened to your boy, Jam Master J! Come to the TV, man!"

I was like, *yeah right*. People are always joking on you and stuff in jail, trying to see if they get something going. I was gonna ignore it, but they kept yelling for me to come. Finally, I went to the TV room, and they were broadcasting what had happened. When they said Jam Master J was dead, something inside me snapped, man. I went ballistic inside that jail, naw'mean? It took the whole jail to calm me down. All the feelings left my body. I was numb.

I did have a little power on "the Island," man, so I sent word to other parts of the jail, and I sent out a hit on the guy that shot Jam Master J. "Whoever this guy is, if he comes through here, you know what to do" is what I told 'em. I had friends all over the Island. The wire went round the whole jail and came back, "We got you, Flav. We got you."

If we don't get that dude, the streets are gonna get him, I know that for sure. The next morning from jail, I was live on HOT 97, talking about Jam Master J.

Losing J put a hole in rap music. I kept thinking about him and me, sitting on the back of that tour bus, making pause button tapes. I thought of being on stage with him and so many good times.

I didn't go to funeral. I couldn't. I was locked up, but I want to tell his family that I would have been there for them if I could have been, and I know that God's looking out for them.

Not going to that funeral was just one more thing drugs cost me, man.

The last time I did jail time was for moving violations. I had a bunch of them and New York state law says that if you get stopped for eleven moving violations, on the twelfth one, you gotta go to jail—period. I got busted for driving with no license—about 68 times.

Now, about me and a drivers' license. I haven't had a driver's license in New York since 1983 when I was working for a school bus company. Yeah, that's right. Your boy had a Class 2 license and used to drive a big yellow school bus! I had an accident with my school bus, and the cops took my license and told me I could get it back if the school bus company filed some paperwork and did a hearing on whether the accident was my fault or not. The school bus company never responded, and then they went out of business. I was gonna respond to that stuff on my own, but it took me so long to get the paperwork together. I didn't have a copy of the accident report, and finally, when I never responded to the hearing, they revoked my license. So, it wasn't that your boy was speeding or driving reckless or nothing like that. I just kept getting caught driving with no license.

Well, I was usually speeding or something, and that's how they *found out* I didn't have no license.

I kept getting caught driving without a license and the twelfth time, they locked me up. Well actually, that last time, there was a little more to it. I was on the Southern State Parkway in my 'Vette heading from the Bronx to Roosevelt, doing 130 mph in a 55 mph zone. I looked in the rear view and I saw the police coming after me waaaayyyyy back in the distance. I could have gotten away from them if I wanted to, but I pulled over and waited for them like a dumb ass 'cause I was high and paranoid. I didn't want to get beat the fuck up while high on crack.

That's not a good feeling, Gee. Trust me.

When they pulled me over, I had 68 moving violations. I knew I was going to do time. I spent a night in jail and they set a court date for September 13, 2001.

September 10, 2001, though, I wasn't even in New York. I was in Atlanta with Chuck D, trying to work on some music. We created two records, "Flavor Man" and a tune called "Can a Woman Make a Man Lose His Mind?"

I had to get back to New York for that court date on September 13. I was supposed to leave on the 10th, but the weather was bad—rain, dark, heavy clouds and lightning. All the planes were grounded until the weather cleared.

I stayed at the airport with a girl that I met from the Bronx, waiting. The flights just kept getting more and more delayed.

It was 11:30 p.m. before things cleared and we finally took off.

I arrived in LaGuardia at 3 a.m., took a cab to my place in the Bronx, and got some crack before going home. I smoked until I fell asleep in front of the TV.

When I woke up hours later, there were people running all over the place on the television, screaming. I thought I was watching the news of a bomb gone off in some foreign country, man.

Then I realized it was New York.

They started showing one of the World Trade buildings on fire.

It was crazy.

I jumped up, grabbed my binoculars, and ran to my kitchen window, searching the skyline. I saw what I thought at first was a helicopter. I thought they were trying to do some kind of rescue.

It wasn't a rescue because then I saw a big fireball and smoke filling the air as the second plane hit the second tower.

Wowwww...

I saw those two skyscrapers crumble through my binoculars and then again and again on TV.

Man, that was the most horrifying thing I'd ever seen.

My court date got postponed. For two or three days after the attacks, there were no trains, no phones, and power lines were affected. Most offices were closed.

It was just terrible.

Finally, the courts re-opened. I went to court on September 16th and was sentenced to a mandatory year in jail.

Riker's Island.

It gets worse.

While I was in jail, I got evicted from my apartment at Executive Towers in the Bronx. That happened because of a couple COs who didn't like me and because of that bitch Michelle from the Phoenix House, who was my new probation officer. They basically made sure I never even got a chance to respond to any of the stuff about my apartment until my shit was on the street.

I'm telling you, I hate that woman. I feel like she went out of her way to fuck your boy over. It's just wrong, man.

She knows who she is, and she knows what she did. Payback is a bitch, bitch.

If it hadn't been for my boys, Jack Hamilton and Izzy Weinstock, I don't know what would have happened to the rest of my things, man. They helped me out a whole lot. Most of my stuff had gone into storage. My boy, Steve Skrobolla, paid for trucks to get my stuff and take it out to eastern Long Island where my boy, Jack, had a vacant building where I could store my possessions. When I got out of jail, they helped me get into my last rehab at the LICR- Long Island Center of Recovery. It was a special place for famous people, musicians and shit, tucked away in the Hamptons.

I made some good friends there, like Joey Bartone, (who died in a car accident a while later) and Joey Conan. They were like brothers to me, like family. LICR was a good experience, but even LICR didn't stop me from using, once I was back in the Bronx.

When I got out of jail, I went to Bev, my loving supportive girl who'd held it down for your boy all that time. My Bev, who promised me—swore to me—that she'd never, ever, *ever* turn your boy down if he needed a place to lay his head.

I hadn't been there more than a few weeks when that promise went out the window.

I'll never forget it, Gee. I was sitting on the couch in my drawers. It was early, *early* in the morning, like 5 a.m. or some shit like that, and we were arguing. It was really heated, man. Bev says, "That's *it*. Get the hell out!"

I went and put on my clothes and walked out of the house and that was that. I felt like she'd betrayed me, man. I felt like she'd abandoned her promise, and abandoned your boy.

I felt as bad as I can ever remember feeling, man. I had no money, and I was flat broke. I didn't even have enough money to catch the train out to my mother's house. My brother-in-law, Ronald Lincoln, came out from Long Island to the Bronx to get me.

I was back at my mom's house after that—41 years old and all messed up. I didn't have a girl, I didn't have a gig, and I didn't even have an apartment. I'd been to rehab at least four different times, and I was still a fucking addict.

I'd tried living in Houston and Chicago, trying to get away from the environment that made it just too easy for me to get drugs, and it hadn't helped.

I'd had all kinds of opportunities. Your boy even did the "Geographic Traffic" for New York City's 105.1 radio station when it launched with jocks, Dr. Dre, Ed Lover and Lisa G., but I kept screwing up and relapsing and nothing seemed to last.

Your boy didn't know what to do anymore, so I smoked up whatever little money came my way, hung out with some of my friends from the old days, and kept doing all the things that had brought me to where I was at—broke, addicted, alone and angry.

Finally, I went to 3 Third Place, the address where Chuck D had grown up and had turned into his studio and personal living quarters, to see Chuck and Hank Shockley. "Revolverlutions" was coming out and we were doing a little work on it, but then we started talking about more personal stuff.

I had always kept a lot of what was going on with me from my group, but when I missed shows and stuff, they knew what was going on, naw'mean? Still, I'd known those guys a long time and this time, when I saw them, your boy, Flavor Flav, was talking, man.

I guess maybe I had a feeling that my nine lives were nearly up.

I was talking about being back in Freeport and needing to get out and get my own place. I was thinking Manhattan, maybe in a neighborhood far enough from my old drug places that I wouldn't be as tempted, when Hank said, "Hey man, instead of you getting an apartment in downtown Manhattan, why don't you take that same money and go out to LA and see what you can do there?"

I thought about it and felt that maybe he was right. New York was dragging me down. I knew where to get drugs on the secret and no one would know. I needed to change my people, my places and my things. Manhattan probably wouldn't have been far enough from my old friends and bad habits to keep me clean, but Los Angeles might be.

As I thought about making the move, a little voice inside my head said, "Go. Get the hell out of New York before you end up killing yourself."

I left New York a few weeks later with $142 and a cell phone. That's it. I told myself that I wasn't coming back until I got on TV or in a movie. I told myself I wasn't coming back until I got myself a house in LA and another one in Las Vegas.

As I boarded the plane and felt it jump into the air, man, it was just like the feeling I had when I felt the steps of that ladder come back under my feet after hanging by my arms in that manhole under the 59th Street Bridge. I'd been in the hole. I'd seen what was down there. I'd stared the possibility of my own death square in the face and then, satisfied that death was there, I pulled myself up, climbed up out of the hole and started walking.

I walked away from drugs that day, and I've never looked back.

Thanks, Bev.

PART THREE

Recreating
Flavor Flav

Chapter 17

A Surreal Flavor

"T HAT SHIT IS FOR HAS-BEENS."

That's what I said the first time someone suggested that I should be in the cast of Season 3 of *The Surreal Life* on VH1. I wasn't no has-been, and I didn't want to do it.

But they were asking me to do a TV show, and that was one of my goals for moving to LA in the first place.

To tell the truth, almost as soon as I landed in Los Angeles, things started to change for me.

I met all kinds of new people and friends of old friends who were willing to give your boy, Flavor Flav, a helping hand and a fresh start. Even more important, something changed inside me, too.

I felt *hopeful*, man. I felt like I had a goal again, naw' mean? I knew I wanted to get on a TV show or to be in a movie. I knew I wanted to have my houses and I really wanted to finally release a solo album. I wanted to make my own music again.

I think God made a way for your boy. I *believe* that. I felt it, naw'mean? It was almost like he was saying, "Okay Flav, this is your last shot. It's up to you now. Don't FUCK IT UP."

He put all kinds of people in my life to help me, but He also put the devil there in all forms and fashions to test me to see if I would fail.

First, there was the good stuff. There was my friend Princess Hemphill, who had a one bedroom apartment on Colfax Avenue in North Hollywood, and who let me stay with her there while I got myself together. My boy, Jinx, lived right around the corner from Princess. Jinx was the DJ for Ice Cube and I used to go over to his house all the time. I met this guy named Norris Preston-Rakin who was one of the editors on the show *Steve Harvey's Big Time Challenge*. Norris was like, "Flav, I want you to come the show. Come sit in the audience and let Steve Harvey shout you out!"

We did it. We had snuck in there between acts while it was dark, so no one knew I was there. When they did breaks between parts of the show, all the lights went up and I stood up and hollered out, "Yo, Steve!"

Well, the crowd went wild, and Steve Harvey went wild, too. He had me come up on the stage and he told everyone a story that I had forgotten. He told them that, if it hadn't been for Flavor Flav, there wouldn't be a Steve Harvey. He told them about how, back in the 90s, *Public Enemy* had performed at *Showtime at the Apollo,* but we were running late, so the producers let this young, unknown comic get on the stage to fill the time.

You guessed it. That comic was Steve Harvey! He *killed* that night. There was an agent in the audience who approached Steve, and the rest, as they say, is history, folks.

I really didn't even know that I'd had that kind of impact on Steve's career, but it was nice to hear it and I'm glad for the brother. It just goes to show how a small thing, like *Public Enemy* running late—which I'm sure was my fault, naw' mean—can create an opportunity for someone deserving. It proves that everything happens for a reason. God is good. I really appreciated Norris taking me to *Steve Harvey's Big Time Challenge* that night and giving me the chance to have my first TV appearance. Folks, Flavor Flav has been on TV ever since!

While I was living with Princess Hemphill, every now and then I'd go to this barbershop called Brother 2 Brother. Next door was a hair salon called Diamonds. That's where I met my stylist, Antisa.

I was always funny about who touched my head, and I won't let just anyone braid my hair. Once I find the right person, I'm set. When I moved to Los Angeles, I wanted one person, the same person, to do my hair. I found Antisa, and

by the time I made it to television, I took Antisa with me
and gave her a permanent job as my stylist. Everywhere I
went, and every show I did, Antisa came, too. I wouldn't go
anywhere without her. Anytime you've seen me on TV with
braids, Antisa did it. She kept me looking good. A lot of the
suits I wore on TV, she picked them. She styled the hell out
of your boy—thank you, Antisa!

Okay, I know, I know. I'm getting ahead of myself, but
your boy just has to say "thank you" to Antisa because she
wasn't only my stylist, she's also my friend.

Another thing happened around the same time.

I was standing inside Brother 2 Brother, and this white
guy comes up to me says, "Hey Flav. You know Devonte Swing,
from Jodeci?"

"But, of course," I said. I knew who he was.

So this guy says, "My name is Fido and I work with Devonte."

"Where is he?"

"I can take you to him."

Fido—he's got a name just like a dog, man—took me
out to meet Devonte at his studio. When I got there and
saw Devonte, I was star-struck. I went crazy. I was like head
over heels for my boy, Devonte Swing. We share the same
friend, Cheryl Konigsberg, who happens to be my son, Quanah's, godmother and was also my overseer at Def Jam for
years. When I say "overseer," that's what I mean. I was a fucking nut, man. Cheryl was the only one who could get me to
my gigs. She was the one who made sure that I was where I

needed to be. She got me to do shit that my group couldn't get me to do. She got me to do shit *no one* could get me to do because that's how fucked-up I was. So when I say "overseer," that's exactly what I mean.

Devonte was like, "Flav, if you ever want to work on music, come on down. You don't have to pay nothing. Free for you."

I was like "Wowww...thanks, Gee! I'll be baack!" Just to let y'all know, once I came back, mind you, I did not leave Devonte Swing's studio for two and a half years.

Remember, your boy was pretty much broke when I left New York, so the opportunity to hang out in the studio, make some music and get creative, without having to worry about how much it cost, was very large for me.

I started going to the studio a lot—living there, really. That's where I met Fido's brother, Rome. We got really close, me and Rome. He was the engineer on my solo album—but I'm getting ahead of myself again.

You want to hear about the TV stuff, right?

Okay, folks, here it goes...

Laurie Muslow and Marilyn Gill were the ones who put me on *The Surreal Life.*

There was a woman named Sherry—I can't remember her last name right now—who first took me over to the VH1 office back in 2003. I had come for a meeting about maybe doing some kind of show with them, but instead of going directly into my meeting, I was doing what I do.

You know what *that* means, right?

Your boy was going around the office saying "hello" to everyone, taking pictures and saying "Flavor Flaaavvvvv!"

Like I said, it's what I do. If I come to your office, it's what I'm gonna do. I come to see one person, but you can bet I'm not going to leave until I've greeted everyone.

Me doing what I do, the way I made my presence known the way that I did that day, sort of gave the people at VH1 the idea that I might be good on one of their shows.

I went in again another day, this time to have a meeting with Chris Abrego and Mark Cronin, the creators of *The Surreal Life*, as they were working on casting *Surreal Life 3*.

"Flav," they said. "We'd love to have you join the cast of *Surreal Life 3*. What do you think?"

I knew that *Surreal Life 1 and 2* had had a bunch of people on them who had once been hot in the entertainment game, but who ended up getting cold. I thought it was a show for has-beens and I didn't consider myself a has-been because I was still iconicly huge, naw'mean?

I didn't want to do it.

"Nah, man. That shit's for has-beens."

They really wanted me to do it. They kept trying to persuade your boy, but I still wasn't feeling it.

Finally, someone suggested that I talk to MC Hammer.

Hammer was on the first *Surreal Life*. They gave Hammer a call and put me on the phone with him. Here I am on the phone with MC Hammer and I say, "Yo, Hammer, you think I should do this TV show, man?" and he says, "Yo, Flav, I think it's a great idea, man. Great things can happen for your life after the show. It happened to me, man and it could work for you, too."

Then I said to myself, *"Woww... maybe he's right."*

My goal had been to be on a TV show, or in a movie, and here was a TV show just asking for your boy to be on it. I didn't want to seem like I was a has-been or a D-list celeb, but it's like they say—the (surreal) life is what you make it.

Hee, hee, har, har!

I decided to try it, and I said to myself, *"Hammer, this shit better be good or I'm coming to see you, Gee."*

It turned out to be one of the greatest things I could have done, lettin' MC Hammer talk me into doing *Surreal Life 3*.

Before we did the deal, though, there was one thing the producers wanted to make sure of.

"You're drug free, right, Flav?" they asked me. "Because we don't want to put you on if there's going to be any problems like that."

"Yeah, I'm clean, man," I said and I was, but at that moment, I just made up my mind that I really was going to stay that way.

Just like that, naw'mean?

After almost two decades of drug use and abuse, I was done with that life—*snap*—like that. Moving to LA made a huge difference because I didn't have a network of people and places that I could go to get drugs secretly. The other thing that happened was that I started to see a life for myself that didn't involve using. I started to see opportunities, man. Things I really wanted to do.

Like I said before, I've been to rehabs a bunch of times, but in the end it was just those two things—a big change of scenery and some brand new opportunities—that helped me change my life.

Little did I know that *The Surreal Life* would be the show that set me on the path to a whole new career.

When it was time to start filming the show, I showed up at the Surreal House as scheduled. I knew most of my cast mates, either by sight or reputation. I knew Jordan Knight from *New Kids on the Block* by name, but when I walked in and saw him there, I didn't know exactly who he was. I thought I kinda recognized him, but I hadn't seen him in a long time, like years and years.

See, I used to be good friends with Donnie Walberg, who is one of his band mates. Later, I became friends with Donnie's brother, Mark Walberg, who is now a major movie star, in case you didn't know. He's come a long way from *Marky Mark and the Funky Bunch*, naw'mean? I remember playing basketball with Mark in Australia on some tour back in the day. We were buddies. Wherever you found Mark, you found Flav. I'm so very happy for him and proud of him!

I really did recognize Charo because she used to be on that show from the 1970s, *The Love Boat,* as the coochie-coochie lady. She coochied herself all the way to the bank! Hee hee! Behind all that wiggling and shit, she's a sweet lady. Very kindhearted. I miss being around her.

There was a chick named Ryan Starr, but we weren't close on the show. I did not like Ryan Starr, and Ryan Starr hated Flavor Flav. She had been on *American Idol* and got booted off. She was a used-to-be Idol contestant who found her way to television. She wasn't really even a has-been, man. More like a "never was," naw'mean?

There was my boy, comedian Dave Coulier, from the TV show *Full House*. We became good friends. I didn't know that Dave was on TV because I had never seen *Full House*. I liked him anyway. He's a funny dude.

And of course, I'll never forget when this tall blonde lady came in wearing high heels.

I was standing in the living room and my first thought was, *"This lady is already 6'4" tall, why does she need high heels?"* I kinda recognized her...nah, I'm lying. I didn't have a clue who she was.

Hee, hee, har, har!

Of course, it was Brigitte Neilson, who I ended up falling in love with. For real, yo. Not for TV, not for ratings, and not for fake. Me and Brigitte, that was *for real*.

At first, she didn't like your boy very much, but as we settled in the house, we started to get to know each other and learn each other's habits.

Oh boy, did Brigitte have some habits!

Man!

Brigitte Nielson always walked around that Surreal House butt *naked*. I'm talking totally nude. She *loved* being naked. Everybody had to make adjustments to that because she was going to do it, and it didn't matter that there were other people there, or cameras or anything. Brigitte didn't care what anybody else thought, and that's something that I loved and respected about her. She was walking around with her titties flopping around all over the place, and she has some big, big titties, man. She had absolutely no shame.

I loved it.

One night, Brigitte came into my room and hopped into my bed, naked, of course. Mind you folks, it's been almost two weeks into shooting this show and your boy hasn't had any pussy in *days*. The very worst thing that Brigitte could have done was jump in my bed and I haven't had any pussy in two weeks. The worst. She got in there and covered herself up. Now the thing about the Surreal House is that there are cameras everywhere and at night there are infrared cameras all over. The only places there aren't any cameras are in the bathrooms so you could shower or take a crap or a pee, but everywhere else, everything's on film, naw'mean?

Brigitte's in my bed naked with her big old titties and her big old ass, and your boy, he's getting kinda excited. I told Brigitte, "If you're gonna hop in my bed, we gonna do this thing." We still had to think about the cameras, right? I told her, "You turn your back to me and I..." Well, you know what happened next, folks.

I was like, "Okay, lady. You watch the camera. I got the rest."

I got busy. Her head turned back toward me. She was surprised. The look on her face was like, "Hey, you're big!"

I'm like, "Hey, what did you expect? Tom's thumb?"

Did I mention that I hadn't had any pussy in *days*?

She fell right off the bed and took the blanket with her!

Then, we're *both* naked with the infrared cameras recording us. I didn't want the whole world seeing my joint, so I had to turn myself to wall.

Hee, hee, har, har!

After that night, Brigitte was in love with your boy. She couldn't get enough of your boy, Flavor Flav, after that first night.

Yeaaaahh Boyeee!

She was playing me close after that. I was loving it. I was playing her close, too. We still had a day or two to go before *Surreal Life 3* was done. The producers had planned this activity that took the whole group of us down to San Diego. I wanted to drive and they wouldn't let me, so I got mad.

When I get really mad, all the crazy "Flavor Flav" stuff just shuts down. Once upon a time, I'd go get real high when I felt like that, but now, I just get real quiet and still, which is the exact opposite of my usual personality, naw'mean? Everybody was kind of tiptoeing around me. People never saw me like that and they didn't know what to do. I was in my "Don't fuck with me, man, or else I'm going to fucking cuss you out" mood and the best thing for anyone to do when I'm like that is just get away from me.

At this point, I'm pissed off and not talking, so I guess Brigitte decided she'd go have some fun on her own. She found some guy and started hanging all over him and she even kissed him. She didn't even know him! That made me even madder. I knew she was like that—she's got love for everyone—but we'd gotten close and I felt disrespected.

When we got back, I was still pissed off and not in the mood to deal with the rest of the people in the house. I went out to the yard and got in the hot tub. Well, I'm not in there more than a few minutes when here comes Brigitte, naked, of course. She climbs into the hot tub with me and starts being sweet and stuff. I was holding her, feeling on them big titties and next thing you know.

BOINNNNG!

You know what happened next, folks. We fell in love in that hot tub, too.

Yes, love. Strange as it might be, this six-foot-four inch Danish woman and my skinny black self had real feelings for each other.

By the time the show finished taping, me and Brigitte were a couple and *Surreal Life 3* was VH1's top-rated show in 2004.

Chapter 18

Strange Flavors

WHEN *SURREAL LIFE* ENDED, Brigitte was supposed to go back to Italy, and I was supposed to go back to my place in LA. Instead, we went to the Mandarin Hotel and checked in together. Brigitte missed four planes home! She was about to miss the fifth one, but I made her get out of bed and go home to her family.

I hated to see her go, man, but she's a mom, and she's got kids to look after, naw'mean? She had to go home.

She left, but almost as soon as she was gone, I got a call.

Chris Abrego and Mark Cronin wanted to talk to me. We met, and when our meeting was over the three of us had come up with an idea for Brigitte and me to do a show together.

We were an odd couple, naw'mean? We were so different —tall and short, white and black, European and Long Island...

Hee,hee, har, har!

We were so different looking and different sounding that it was just weird, man. That's what made it interesting.

That's how we came up with *Strange Love*.

My buddy, Matt Odgers, wrote a lot of that show. We made sure that it was both true to what was happening between me and Brigitte and really entertaining, too. The producers were Ben Samek and Matt Odgers, but Ben's assistant, Nicki Nick, Lauren Stevens and Christian (why can't I remember your last name, Christian?) were really helpful, too.

So there I am, in a limousine speeding toward Newark Airport. I'm hanging out the sunroof, hollering "Brigitte, I'm coming I'm going to get you! Brigitte!"

I'll never forget that, driving down the road screaming my head off like that. We put me and the cameras on the plane and flew to Italy. That's where Brigitte and her fiancée, Mattia, were living. They were living together, but I don't think they were engaged then. He was more like her assistant or her butler or whatever. I don't know what she told him, but he had to know something was really going down between us and that this wasn't all just a job for the TV cameras. I feel kinda bad thinking about him. I guess Brigitte ended up just falling for her butler.

We get to Milan and me and those cameras go to their place. I knocked on the door. Mattia answered and he wasn't particularly friendly, because, of course, he knew I was coming to take his girl away from him. It took some dealing, but finally I got Brigitte out of the house and into the car and we drove off to a villa where started taping *Strange Love*. The show hired a nice little old lady to cook and clean for us and make the place like our home.

Then Brigitte took me to meet her family in Europe. It was crazy meeting them. They didn't like me, and they made it clear they weren't *ever* going to like me, not for anything in the world. They didn't understand me. My mannerisms were so far from their perfect manners and they were freaked, man. Brigitte said to her family and friends, "I love this man and I'll be with him no matter what you think."

That's my girl, man.

Then I got to meet Brigitte's kids—Killian, Raoul, and Douglas. The rest of the family might not have liked your boy much, but the kids? They loved me, Gee. That's because your man has a way with kids. I know the way to a child's heart. Usually it's with my sense of humor.

Hee, hee, har, har! Naw'mean?

So we stayed in Italy a few more days, then we went back to America so Brigitte could meet *my* family.

When we arrived, we jumped in a limo and drove out to Roosevelt. She met my mother and my two older sisters. Everybody in Roosevelt and Freeport came to my mother's house that day to meet Brigitte and try to be on TV, naw' mean? It was like a Yankees' game, man. Like Mardi Gras in the streets outside my mother's house when Brigitte came. Everybody was there—I mean *everybody*. People I hadn't seen or thought about in *years*.

Unlike how her family felt about your boy, Brigitte was well-accepted by my family and well-loved in my neighborhood. After she met the fam, we went to the Bronx. I took Brigitte to my ex-girlfriend, Beverly Johnson's, house. She met Bev and her family, and we had a great time. Bev cooked up dinner and her mother, Gina, and my stepkids, Jason and Jasmine Rodriguez, who I still love and consider my children, were there. It made a good show because it was all for real, naw'mean?

Since we were in the Bronx...

I took Brigitte up to Fordham Road to the little shop where I get my gold teeth made and had her fitted for her grill!

Once again, folks, it was crowded! People were all over the place, trying to get a glimpse of me and Brigitte while the cameras were rolling for the show. We had to get a police escort out of there, man. That's how many fans there were in the Bronx that day. It was unbelievable. It was one of the best days of my life, being in the Bronx with Brigitte Neilson.

Later, when the teeth were ready and she put those gold caps on over her real teeth, they got stuck! She couldn't get them off. You should have seen it—it was so funny, man. She was trying to pry them off and they weren't budging! I was laughing my ass off.

It worked out that while we were filming *Strange Love* in New York, *Public Enemy* had a performance scheduled. I took Brigitte with me.

Woowwww...

It was uncomfortable to be performing with *Public Enemy*, which was a pro-black rap group, while I'm dating this white woman. Then, during the show, I called Brigitte out on the stage with us. That probably looked really strange and really unusual to have this tall white chick out there with a militant black group. I didn't care what people thought of me. I was showing unity, man. I was sending out a sign of racial harmony, naw'mean? Of racial barriers being broken down.

I really think that was big on my part.

My group didn't agree. They felt funny about Brigitte being on the stage with us. She *did* look out of place. I was the one trying to make her "in place," which might have been a mistake. Like I said, I didn't care.

That same night, as we were on the stage, someone broke into my dressing room and stole my money, about $2,000, out of my pants pocket. When I discovered that the money was gone, I turned into another person, man. I went ballistic. I was tearing the dressing room apart, cussing, yelling and the whole nine.

Brigitte got really upset. I guess I must have scared her really bad, because she started crying and shit. She kept saying, "Please, stop, Foofy, please. Calm down…" over and over.

I wasn't having it.

I hate thieves. I hate stealing, and I ought to 'cause I've done plenty of it in my past. Ever since I stopped using drugs and cleaned up my life, I run it straight and narrow, man. Stealing isn't in my present or my future, naw'mean? I have grown up a lot since those days. I've asked God's forgiveness for that, and I've come to a better appreciation of what's right, so being a victim of a thief? Man, that really pissed me off.

Brigitte could say, "Calm down, Foofy," all she wanted. The only thing that was gonna calm me down was finding out who took my shit and beating his ass!

Speaking of our nicknames...

I call Brigitte "Gitte" because that's her real name. That's the name her moms gave her on the day she was born. "Brigitte" is more of her stage name. She started calling me "Foofy" when she was trying to translate "Flavor Flav" into Italian. Truth is, there is no translation for your boy, Flavor Flav—I'm Flavor in 160 languages!

Hee, hee, har, har!

Seriously, folks, she was fooling around with the translation and came up with "Foofy-foofy" and it stuck. I thought it was kinda crazy but, okay.

As quickly as our relationship got started, it started to lose steam, naw'mean? By the time we left New York for Vegas, we were in a rocky place. We stayed at the Hard Rock Hotel and Casino, but we were getting tired. Brigitte had gotten sick in New York and we'd had to stop production to wait for her to get better. I think we were both realizing that things weren't going to work out between us.

The producers had planned a skit for us at the airport where Brigitte boards a plane and flies off without me. I knew that's what we were going to do, and even though Brigitte and I had kinda moved on, I still cared a lot about her. I knew she was going back to Italy to marry Mattia and that I wouldn't be seeing her much anymore, so I really was sad.

"There goes my love!" I said when that plane took off with Brigitte on it. I cried like a baby—I really did. I felt like all the love I had for Gitte was coming up right then, Gee, so I really was upset. They took me back to the hotel and I just wanted to be quiet by myself for a minute, naw'mean?

What I didn't know was that the plane had turned around and come back. The producers had snuck Gitte back into the hotel. I knew her plane was going to take off and all that, but I really *didn't* know there was more coming. When I got back to the hotel and all of her stuff was there, I was like, "What's going on?" Then she came out of the other room and it was like woww!

The producers didn't tell me about that part because they wanted my real reactions. They knew I wasn't faking my feelings for Brigitte and that our connection to each other was real, naw'mean? By tricking me like that, they brought all that real stuff out again. It was one emotional day for your boy.

Their little trick was good TV, but it didn't change the bottom line. Brigitte lived in Italy and I lived in America. Her family was in Italy and mine was here. Our relationship had ended before the show did, but we still had real love for each other. Still do. But Brigitte married Mattia and that was that.

Strange Love was VH1's number one show that year, but your boy, Flavor Flav, was alone. Having been involved with two number one shows for VH1, it wasn't long before I was in another meeting with Mark Cronin and Chris Abrego to try to come up with another show. They said to me, "Hey Flav, you ever seen *The Bachelor*?"

I said, "I've heard of it, but I've never watched it."

They said, "Very good, Flav. How would you like to have 25 girls all to yourself? And you can pick and choose which-ever ones that you want?"

I said, "Great! Let's do it. I can give that a try."

Then they said to me, "Okay, Flav. We're gonna put you in a house with 25 girls, but you have to eliminate them down to only one."

"What the hell," I said. "Bring on the girls, man!"

Not only did they bring on the girls, man, they also gave me someone else that was fantastic to my show and to my life—Big Rick. Big Rick was my limo driver and assistant on the *Flavor of Love* shows. He helped keep the peace in that house, because I gotta tell you folks, some of those girls ended up being crazy, naw'mean?

With Big Rick and house full of girls picked out, we were all set.

Then something completely unexpected happened. Between the end of *Strange Love* and the beginning of *Flavor of Love 1*, I went to the American Music Awards in Las Vegas and I met Liz, my fiancée. It was love, almost from first sight.

Chapter 19

The Real Flavor of Love

S HE WAS STANDING BY HERSELF, looking a little lost.
It was at the Monte Carlo Hotel and Casino in Las
Vegas in 2004. Like I said, the American Music Awards had
been held there, and there were a lot of people around. The
place was loud, seriously loud, man. I was hyped up from the
event and all that, but I saw this woman with a lot of long,
dark hair piled up on her neck and a cute little shape to her
body. She was sort of standing at the edge of the lobby, looking like she was waiting for something.

I was like, "Everybody, shut the fuck up!" and I pointed at
her. "You! Come over here!"

She couldn't believe I was talking to her. She kinda looked around a little like, "Who, me?"

Then finally, she walked over to me.

I said to her, "Hey, what's your name?"

"Liz," she said.

I said, "What you doin', relative? Would you like to come with me? I'm going to a party for Paris Hilton and you're coming with me."

Before she could give me answer, I grabbed her by the hand and we were on our way out the door.

We spent the next few days together hanging out and getting to know each other. Turns out we had met years and years before, when she and a friend came back stage at a *Public Enemy* concert when she was 16. I really didn't remember her, but there was something about her that seemed a little familiar.

The rest is history. We've been together ever since.

I didn't tell her what I was doing on television, and while I was doing the *Flavor of Love* shows, I had Liz in the back of my mind the whole time.

That's my confession about the *Flavor of Love* shows, folks: I wasn't really looking for love, man. I'd already found it.

Meanwhile, your boy was doing good on his goals for moving to California.

I'd been on two television shows—both hits. Check one.

I had a house in Los Angeles and a place in Las Vegas. Check two.

I hadn't released a solo album, but I'd made some good contacts and was working on my music when I could. Sorta check three.

Mostly, I'd been able to stay away from the drugs that had just about ruined me back in New York.

Super check.

Now, I was gonna do this new show, *Flavor of Love,* and I was excited and nervous.

I really love doing TV, man. It's a lot of fun and the reality shows were just another place where I could do what I love—perform and make people laugh and cry, naw'mean? I was excited.

I was nervous, too, because of Liz. I had met this great girl, and I knew I wanted to be with her, but the show meant that I had to entertain all these other girls and pretend like one of them would be my girlfriend at the end.

Now one thing about your boy, Flavor Flav, is that I don't really like to hurt people's feelings, naw'mean? We hadn't been filming *Flavor of Love* too long before I knew that some of these girls were really serious. They were for real. Some of them were really falling for me and I had to be mindful of their feelings, but most of 'em just wanted to be on TV or to see if they could connect with the big bucks that I had my pocket and in my bank account.

Hee, hee, har, har!

In the 'hood, almost everyone has a nickname, and since I couldn't remember the girls' real names anyway, the producers decided I should give everyone of them a name that I could remember. That's how the "Flavor Naming Ceremony" started out, and yes, your boy came up with every name himself.

For me, one of the most memorable things that happened that first season was when this girl, Hottie, who had ginormous titties, made my mother a raw chicken.

My mother came to the *Flavor of Love* house to meet the girls and to advise me on who to eliminate next, right? One of their challenges was to see who could make the best chicken. Flavor Flav *loves* chicken, and I make some serious chicken wings. More on that later, but on that show, I asked the girls to make me a chicken dish.

Well, you saw it.

This girl, Hottie, had these big, big titties, but she had no brains. This girl took a raw chicken, decorated it with carrots and celery, put it in the microwave, pressed the word "chicken" (like for chicken nuggets) and put the chicken in there. The chicken cooked for two minutes and she put it on a plate and served it to my mother.

My mother took one look at it and nearly had a heart attack. This dumb girl served a raw chicken to my mother!

Hottie's brains were in her titties—no joke.

Now, I know what you want to know.

You want to know about when Pumkin spit on New York!

Hee, hee, har, har!

Okay so that was one of the final elimination ceremonies and the only girls left were Hoopz, New York and Pumkin. Things got really heated with the girls. You guys only saw a tiny bit of it. It takes a real long time to film those ceremonies, and while they were setting up cameras and lights and moving things around, Pumkin, Hoopz and New York were arguing with each other. New York and Pumkin hated each other, just hated each other, Gee! They were arguing and calling each other names every time the cameras were off. When it was time for me to make my decision, I eliminated Pumkin. Well, she was still arguing with New York. New York was saying, "Yeah, bitch. Hit me, hit me."

Well, you saw it. Pumkin spit on her and that shit almost went into New York's mouth. New York grabbed Pumkin and smashed her head into the camera!

I was shocked, but I was also cracking up inside, jack! It was great! It became one of the most memorable scenes in reality TV history. To this day, it's one of the top moments on TV. Hoopz was just standing there laughing. I wanted to laugh, too. I probably did, but they just cut that part out.

Everybody in the place was trying to hold New York back. She was mad! That girl is no joke. She is *exactly* like she came across on camera. Very bossy, bitchy and crazy. Her mother, Sister Patterson, is exactly like she seems on TV, too. The woman is all drama.

When I met New York's parents that first time, it was obvious that Sister Patterson didn't like your boy, and that she didn't like me with her daughter. That day, me and New York's father were on the tennis court playing, and her mother was sitting in the corner of the court drinking coffee. To this day, I regret not sending a tennis ball flying in her direction to knock the coffee cup out of her hand or something! I didn't like this lady, and she didn't like me.

I had my chance and I didn't take it.

New York didn't care what her mom thought. She wanted her man and she stuck to me, even though her moms was totally against me.

After I eliminated Pumkin, it was down to New York and Hoopz. We went to Mexico for the shoot of the finale. I knew New York really liked me and that she was down for me, but I didn't pick her.

Why?

Well, folks, you know your boy. He's gonna go for the finest woman he can! Hoopz was the finest. I *had* to end up with Hoopz!

New York was furious. She started cursing me out and all that. I definitely wasn't her friend right then, yo.

For the record, all of the eliminations were made by me alone, with no producer input and that shit. Me.

It worked, too, because *Flavor of Love* was VH1's number 1 show that season. That was three times your boy had been in a number one show on VH1. I was getting it in!

Flavor of Love 2

The girls I remember the most from the second season of *Flavor of Love* are Somthin', Buckey, Krayzee, Buckwild, Myammee, Hotlanta—and of course, Deelishis.

The first season of the show had been tough. Like I said, I wasn't really looking for love as much as *dough*, but the second season it was even tougher. I was thinking of Liz back in Vegas and doing the show felt very awkward. I guess I didn't make the show all it could have been because of that.

I ain't gonna forget when that girl, "Somthin'," shitted on the floor during the elimination ceremony, that's for sure.

All the girls were all on the elimination stand, waiting for me to choose who was staying in the house and who was going home. Somthin' had to go to the bathroom, but the producers wouldn't let her. As I've said before, those elimination ceremonies take a long time to shoot, so it was hours they were standing there. She had drunk a lot that day, and she ate a lot that day, and her body couldn't hold it anymore. Finally the shit hit the fan.

Hee,hee, har, har!

Somthin' let loose a *huge* turd on the floor which she picked up and tried to hide by smearing it onto the floor with the back of her hand. When the elimination ceremony finally ended, she ran upstairs and left it there.

Folks, I was smelling something foul. It smelled like shit. I thought we had a dog in the house and it had shit. Some of these girls...well, I wouldn't have been that surprised if someone had smuggled a dog in there. I was going up the stairs to my room and I saw this lump of shit on the stairs, and I said, "This is human shit, not dog shit."

A few of the girls were nearby and they told me that Somthin' had taken a dump and run up the stairs.

I went upstairs to see if Somthin' was all right. Deelishis came with me. Deelishis knocked on the door and when the door opened, the smell that came out of that bathroom was so stink you could smell it through the TV.

Wooowww...now that's some stinking shit!

I didn't eliminate her right away, but you know I wasn't gonna keep a girl who would leave a turd on the stairs around for too long.

We brought New York back on the show that season because I thought it would be great television, but emotionally, I knew I was gonna have to be careful. Like I said, I didn't want to hurt anyone's feelings. I also didn't want to lose my girl at home. The other girls didn't like it that New York was back, but there wasn't anything that they could do about it. It was my show. They had to deal with it.

I knew I was acting, but I don't think those girls had a clue what was acting and what was for real. They believed what they wanted to believe, no matter how I acted.

The final two were New York and Delishis. We shot that finale in Belize and, once again, the girls were arguing on the

elimination block. As I was walking to the set to start shooting, I could hear them. It was heated before we even started,
man. Then it was time for me to decide.

New York or Deelishis.

Deelishis or New York.

Then finally, I made my decision.

Deelishis!!!

Why? Boy, oh boy! Have you seen that ass, man?

Hee, hee, har, har!

When I picked Deelishis, New York went nuts! Talk about
showing your ass! She mooned me on camera and then
stormed away. Seriously, New York is a sweet girl, but damn!
She's crazier than a motherfucka. Whatever she was feeling,
she was definitely real with it, man. When she's mad, she's
another *person,* yo! When she showed me her ass like that, I
was laughing. New York may have a nice ass, but she's no real
live Deelishis! I was like, "You can moon me all you want, but
I got the biggest ass in the business right by my side!" Deelishis has an ass that is every man's *dream,* naw'mean?

Then, the show was over and I was on my way back to
Vegas to my girl, Liz. Only at this point, no one really knew
anything about Liz. I knew. Liz was pregnant with our son,
by then, and I needed to get home to her.

Well, that was sort of a problem.

Deelishis, she's thinking she's my girl and all that, but the
chemistry between me and Deelishis wasn't matching up.

She liked me for real, but I had Liz at home and when the cameras shut off, so did my feelings about Deelishis. I still liked the size of her ass, but not enough to risk what I had at home. I was trying to be careful not to hurt Deelishis, but I guess I did anyway.

Liz wasn't too happy either. While I was away taping the *Flavor of Love 2, Flavor of Love 1* was on television. I told Liz not to watch it, and before I left home, I had the cable cut off so she *couldn't* watch it. The biggest mistake I could have made was leaving her with a large sum of money because after I left, she went and cut the bitch back on anyway and watched it! Hee, hee, har har!

Of course, we started having problems. She changed toward me because she was worried about me with all those women. If she'd known from the beginning that I was doing a dating show, I know we never would have been together at all.

She had real issues with it, man. Real issues. She had an issue with the whole concept of the show and real issues with me doing it. She felt like it gave me an excuse so I could cheat on her, but I thought of it as just my job. Still, I wasn't happy that my show bothered her so much. I was so in love with her that when she hurt, I hurt. When she cried, I cried. I regretted the hurt I brought her with those shows, and I still do. Liz is so sweet and smart, and so loving and caring. She's also a very moral person, and a very faithful person.

She kept saying she felt that I used the show to cheat.

I didn't cheat.

I wanted a TV career. I wanted to make money to spend with Liz and the rest of my family. My doing the *Flavor of Love* shows bought her a home, and took care of my kids back in New York. Yeah, I spent time with those girls and I kissed a few of them, but I always ended up back at home with Liz. To me it was just a TV show. It was just entertainment, and I'm an entertainer. She thought it was real, and she didn't believe that I was acting.

The finale of *Flavor of Love 2* was the biggest show ever in the history of non-network cable television with 7.55 million viewers tuning in, the largest numbers VH1 had ever seen. I think it might be a while before they see those numbers again, too. The only one that can bring those numbers back or break my record is *me*. I don't think nobody else can do it. If I were to go back on VH1 right now, I think I'd get 5 million viewers plus again, too. Ray J got close to beating me. He rocked the house with his show and brought in a lot of viewers, but not as many as Flavor Flav. Bret Michaels brought in good numbers, too, but not as good as Flavor Flav.

VH1 ought to give me an award in my own special category for the kinds of numbers I've brought them in viewers! Nah, I don't want no award. Just write me a nice, fat check!

Hee, hee, har, har!

While I'm really proud of all that, I've got to say that I wasn't excited at all about doing *Flavor of Love 3*.

Flavor of Love 3

I didn't want to do it, but I had to do it. I was under contract for three seasons. Liz was torn up by it. I was only in it for the money at this point. VH1 and these shows, starting with the *Surreal Life* and through *Strange Love* and *Flavor of Loves*, had really changed my life, and I was grateful. I kept thinking about how much my life had changed since Bev had kicked me out of her apartment in the Bronx. If I were still there, I'd still be getting high. When Bev kicked me out and I moved back to my mother's house, she set the wheels in motion.

Thanks, again, Bev!

What can say about Season 3?

Remember, this is a *job* for your boy. It's entertainment, right? By the time we got to Season 3, I really wasn't that into it anymore. I had kinda moved on in my mind. It got to be harder to tell the girls apart and to keep myself interested, especially knowing how things were at home because of the show.

There was another thing that was bugging me out about it.

Being on TV dating show, especially three times, paints a very narrow picture of you. It makes you seem like you can't get nobody, even if you *have* somebody. It kinda gets hard on your spirit after a while, being seen that way. I didn't like seeing myself that way, but I had a job to do, so I was going to do it. If it meant pretending to be a lonely celeb sorting through a bunch of chicks, your boy was gonna give it his best shot!

Here are my highpoints from Season 3:

My girl, Shy, was another one who had some stink issues. She was from Chi town and, on a date with her, I couldn't help but notice that her breath was bad. Crazy bad. Her breath was so stank, I was offering her gum, Life Savers, anything I could, man. Nothing helped. She had a rotten tooth in her mouth or something.

It was too bad. She was real and she was real cool and I liked her. It was her breath that I didn't like so much.

That date with Shy was at an aquarium in Los Angeles where we got to jump into a pool with sand sharks. Boyeee, that was the scariest thing in this life for your boy! My nuts got so cold and numb! Wowww....I was scared they were done for. I got out and left Shy in there, naw'mean?

Flavor Flav ain't swimming with no more sharks! Never again. No way. Those fish can feel your fear, man...no, I don't want them biting me up. Nah, man. I got kids!

We went to Paris for the finale and your boy, Flavor Flav, had to decide between Black and Thing 2. I chose Thing 2, even though I was pretty sure she was a gold digger, because she'd been the most down with your boy on the show. Hell, it didn't matter anyway. As soon as we got back to the States, I went back to Liz and when we got to the Reunion show, I knew I was going to tell Thing 2 that it wasn't gonna happen, and that I was in love with my son's mother. Liz was the one I was going to be with.

Oh, I didn't tell you I had a son?

Yeah, I got seven kids. Karma Kahlil Jonathan Drayton was born in 2007, just after *Flavor of Love 3* finished shooting. Once again, your boy was involved in the whole thing, or as much as I could be when I wasn't doing the show. I want three more. I always said I wanted ten kids, but first, I gotta talk Liz into it.

Hee, hee, har, har!

Yo, man, you wanna hear something really strange?

My first born daughter with Karren Ross, Shanique, was born in February. Our son, William, Jr., or "Man" as we call him, was born in March, and our second daughter, Karren, was born in April. They are all one year apart. After me and their mother, Karren Ross, split up, I met up with Angie Parker. Me and Angie have a daughter together, Da'Zyna, and she was born in February. Then we had a son, Quanah, who was born in March, and then we had Kayla, who was born in April! They're all two years apart. And, yo, check this out. The craziest thing is my first two oldest daughters are in February, my two sons are in March, and my last two daughters are in April. There's six years between Karren and D'Zyna, there's seven years between Man and Quanah and there's eight years between Karren and Kayla. Ain't that crazy? I don't know how God did that, but he definitely worked it! It was pretty cool little streak there.

Now here comes my last born, lucky Karma. His birthday is December 26, the day after Christmas. The reason why I say he's lucky is because I think it's very cool to have a birthday right after Christmas. He's now four years old.

Okay, back at the ranch, or rather, I guess I should say, "Back at VH1..." At the Reunion for Season 3, not only did I tell Thing 2 that I couldn't be with her, I brought Liz and Karma onto the show and proposed to Liz on the spot. I was happy because I was able to have my family on TV with me, but Thing 2 was *furious*, man. She felt hurt that her connection with money was over. She wasn't really for me, and like I said, I felt that all along. She was looking for a Sugar Daddy, but once the show was over, so was her time with Flav. I didn't love her. All that was just for television, man.

That was the messiest Reunion of all of them, and that's saying something because all of the *Flavor of Love* Reunions were *crazy*! That last one was messy because Thing 2's whole family was furious with your boy. They felt like they'd been gypped or something and so they came back stage and headed to my trailer. They met up with Liz and started telling her a bunch of garbage, man. They were telling her that I was taking Thing 2 places and doing things with her that I wasn't doing. Anything to mess up my relationship, naw'mean? I guess Thing 2 was like, "If I can't have him, no one can."

Have you seen that mess she and her ex-boyfriend put up about me on YouTube? Bashing me to anyone who will listen and shit. All right, lady. If that's the only way you've got to get over your hurt at losing your boy, then you just do what you got to do.

It didn't change *nothing* in my world. Not one thing. No matter what she said, no matter what her momma said, her daddy, her sister, her ex-boyfriend—whatever, I *still* didn't love her, I still got paid and I still got my family today.

I know there are people who don't like me. I know there are people who don't like what I do. I know there are people who've got all kinds of negative comments to make and shit to say. Mostly, I don't pay them any mind.

See, I had to do what I did to become what I have become. I wouldn't be an icon if I didn't do what I've done the way I've done it, so they can say whatever they want, I don't care. I shrug it off and keep going. They ain't me, and they ain't living in my skin. I wish everyone lived life like me. I don't mind everybody else's business, but everybody else minds mine!

The only thing I ever heard about me that bothered me was when Chris Rock said, "I'll pay the legal fees of anybody who kills Flavor Flav."

That shit hurt my feelings. He was one of my favorite comedians until he said that shit. I took that one personally, man. I know he's a comedian, but I'm supposed to be his boy. That was the second time that he did a joke about me. The first one was at the time when I was struggling with drugs while Darryl Strawberry was struggling, too. The joke was something like:

"Flavor Flav bought a crack pipe from Darryl Strawberry at an auction."

I didn't like that one either, but I shrugged it off.

The killing joke was too much, though. What if someone had really tried to kill me? Hey, I got kids. I got a family and I got a right to live, too, naw'mean?

I've never once lashed out at Chris Rock, or anyone else who criticized me, but I don't like jokes like that. They're not funny.

There was a time when me, Chris Rock, Bill Stephney and Nelson George used to sit in an office and talk about putting projects together. That was before Chris bought his red and black Corvette. He was still living in Brooklyn. After working together like that, I thought we were boys. I thought we were friends.

I never thought he'd strike me like that.

God taught me to forgive, but I don't forget. I'm a forgiving person, and I would accept an apology. The guy has come a long way. The part in *New Jack City* that Chris Rock played was originally supposed to be played by me until Chuck and Hank told the people that created the movie that they didn't want me playing the part of a crack addict because of what *Public Enemy* stood for in terms of no drugs and no alcohol.

Chuck and Hank held me back because they knew that *Public Enemy* couldn't succeed without its hype man. If I'd had a career in the movies, that would have been the end of the group, probably.

That's why they did it. I know it is. If I'd played that part I might have been a movie star.

Who knows?

People ask me all the time if I watched myself on TV. Nah, man. I never saw any of the shows—not *Surreal Life*, *Strange Love*, or any of the *Flavor of Loves*. As soon as we were done taping, it was over to me. I'd go back on tour or back to my life, and that was that.

I never saw *Charm School* or *I Love Money* or any of the shows that spun off my shows. I did see a little of *I Love New York*—your boy was curious, just like everyone else—but not much of it. I don't watch much television, period. Got too much else going on, man. Still, I was happy for New York that she had her own show. I was happy that I could help build careers for other people and provide them with a "break" into television, naw'mean?

Now, here's some behind the scenes shit for you:

VH1 would love to have me do another reality type show, probably like Flav and New York, or some shit, but I can't. I'm in a real relationship and I'm happy in it. I'm not willing to do that for money unless my girl was with it and understood it was completely fake. Since that's not how she sees it,

I just can't do it. Yeah, I might make some money, but when I came back home, my family would be gone.

Besides, after almost five years in reality TV, I was really ready to try something completely different.

Under One Roof
(2008 TV series)

Reality TV had helped me climb out of one of the deepest holes I've ever found myself in my life. I got so busy with TV projects that I just stopped messing with crack. TV helped me do what no rehab could. Your boy was finally "just saying no" to drugs.

Still, Flavor Flav is a daredevil, naw'mean? Adventurous, that's me. Since I'd already been in a few movies—remember me in *Mo' Better Blues* and *New Jack City*, and if you haven't seen them, check me out in *Confessions of a Pit Fighter* and *Cain and Abel*—when the chance came to do a sitcom, I figured, what the heck? How different could it be from what I'd already done?

Well...

It was called *Under One Roof* and was created by Claude Brooks and Darryl Quarles. The original pitch was for Flavor Flav and Gary Coleman to play a couple of brothers who are really different—one is really successful and conservative and the other is Flavor Flav!

Hee, hee, har, har!

Seriously, folks, one brother's really straight and the other, the one I play, is an ex-convict who is really wild and crazy and all like that.

Man, so let me tell you...

The day of the first meeting about putting the show together, they had me come out and Gary Coleman come out and wowwwww....I got star struck, man. Really, really star-struck, naw'mean? I was so excited. I couldn't believe I was sitting in the room with the guy from *Diff'rent Strokes,* a little midget movie star. We became good friends. He didn't get the show because of his kidney problems. He was on dialysis, which prevented him from shooting on the schedule they needed. I was kinda disappointed about that. I would've loved to work with him.

They decided to use another actor, a young brother named Kelly Perine. Kelly has done a lot of work in television, and a few movies, too, but a lot of stuff on television, particularly sitcoms. He was on *Hangin' with Mr. Cooper* and a show called *Between Brothers.* He was on *The Parent 'Hood* and *The Drew Carey Show* and another show called *One on One.* That's just a few. My boy's done a lot of TV work over the years. He's a real pro, naw'mean?

I didn't know who the hell he was.

Hee,hee, har, har! Like I said, I don't watch much TV.

During the shooting, we became very, very good friends. Your boy has been in movies and done reality shows, but I never really learned anything much about acting. Up to then, I hadn't ever really had to do much "real" acting, naw'mean? I was always playing some version of myself, but this was a little different because, although Calvester Hill (the character I played on *Under One Roof*) was a lot like me, he clearly wasn't me. Doing that sitcom was the first time I really had to focus on the role and the character in a consistent way. Yeah, Kelly taught me a lot. He helped me enhance my role. Thank you, Kelly, for teaching me. Maybe me and you will do some future projects together. I also owe a lot to my boy, Michael Ralph, who was my acting coach for the *Under One Roof* project. I learned so much from Michael, who had been on *The Bernie Mac Show*, playing the part of one Bernie's best friends for years.

We had a great cast—Carrie Ginsell, Marie Michel, Jesse Reid, Emily Kuroda Kelly and your boy. The whole season, all 13 episodes were shot in Vancouver Canada, in a city called Colquitlam, because it was cheaper than shooting in LA. I had a ball up there, shooting in Colquitlam. There was a Greek restaurant that I used to go to so much that the owner and I got to be friends. We'd eat and then go in the back and smash plates on the floor, man. Your boy had a plate-smashing frenzy, naw'mean? Breaking plates everywhere, and not getting in trouble for it? Man, it was the *best!*

Darryl Quarles did some of the writing, but there were a couple of other writers, too. It just seemed like Claude

Brooks, the producer, didn't want to spend the money to have a large enough writing staff to make the show as funny as it could have been. I mean, Darryl had written for *The Fresh Prince* and for Martin Lawrence's *Big Mama's House*, so he had the chops, naw'mean?

We all thought the show could make it, but it didn't happen. The show fell through after the first 13 episodes. There wasn't a second season, which damaged me financially because I had just built a house in Las Vegas, something I dreamed of when I left New York six years before, and I was really counting on the money from a second season to finish it.

It didn't happen.

I was stuck. I didn't have a new project lined up, so I had to struggle a bit. Like a lot of people in late 2008 and 2009, I got pinched a bit financially. At one point, I was a little worried that your boy and his family were going to lose that brand new place, but then I had to remember I still had my group, *Public Enemy*. With *Public Enemy*, I could still make money to keep up with my place, so I didn't have to struggle so hard.

Comedy Central Roast

I haven't said anything about my roast.

Your boy, Flavor Flav, was roasted by Comedy Central and it was one of the most funnest times in my life, man. It was one of the most watched roasts in the history of roasts. I got made fun of by Snoop Dogg, Brigitte Nielsen, Katt Williams, Jimmy Kimmel, Jeff Ross, Sommore, Carrot Top, Lisa Lampanelli, Greg Giraldo, Patton Oswalt, and Ice-T. The coolest thing was when they put me in that harness and lifted me up in the air on a conveyor belt. There I was, flying over the audience right up to the stage. The crowd loved it. They were going *wild,* naw'mean?

After flying across the theater like that, Katt Williams was on the stage to un-harness me and escort me to my throne, then immediately he starts making fun of me. That was my first time ever having been to a roast and I didn't know what to do with it. Everyone else was funny, but I don't think I was funny. It took me the whole show to understand that a "roast" is just playing the dozens!

I've been playing the dozens my whole life! No one beats your boy at playing the dozens. Playing the dozens is how I first hooked up with Chuck and Hank and ended up being part of *Public Enemy*!

I want a "Roast of Flavor Flav, Part Two" so I can throw some serious, serious snaps in!

Chapter 20

Future Flavors

D OING THOSE TV SHOWS opened up a whole new world for me. I accomplished all the goals I set out for myself when I left New York, and more.

That's not the end of the story, folks! Your boy, Flavor Flav, has a lot more ideas, a lot more plans, and a lot more ambitions. I got a bunch of TV and movie projects rolling, and some of them are coming soon to a screen near you.

Yahoo and Friends

Your boy, Flavor Flav, is the voice of "Father Time" in the cartoon series called *Yahoo and Friends,* launching later this year. It's for kids, it's environment-oriented, and it's fast-paced and funny. I love cartoons, and it's exciting to be asked to be a character in one. I can imagine sitting with my son,

Karma, watching *Yahoo and Friends* and he'll be looking at me and looking at the screen wondering how my voice can come out of the character while I'm sitting there with him! Buggin' out!

Hee,hee, har, har!

It's the project of my friends at Levy Productions and you'll be seeing it on a station near you some time in 2011.

More Reality

There's *Flavor Flav Goes Back to High School* almost coming soon. It's more of a reality show thing, but the idea is for real. I want to go back and get my diploma. I want this television show to influence people my age and say to them that it's never too late to go back. After all, if I can do it, you can do it.

I hope the show will also speak to kids who are in school right now. I want to say to them, "Get your diploma now, while you have the chance. Don't wait until you're old like me because you might not make it back to school to get it. Just go on and get it now while you're young and then you can move on with your life."

One day, I'd love to star in my own movie, too. I have a couple of projects in the works. My friend Bryan Holt (who's from Roosevelt like me, but who moved out here to LA), and his partner Reed, have written two movies for me. One is called *Macula* and it's a remake of *Blackula* with a little of the *Night of the Living Dead* and *Chain Saw Massacre* in it, too. We took the movie *Blackula* and crossed it with a movie called *The Mac*. I am Macula and you know, of course, that back in the day, "macking" was another form of "pimping," right?

Hee,hee, har, har!

The other script is sort of a spinoff of my *Flavor of Love* shows, called *Kill to Love You*. I can't tell you anymore about it. It would spoil the surprise...plus, Bryan and Reed would kill me! Then I couldn't make the movie, could I?

Hee, hee, har, har!

Building the Brand

I got my fingers in all kinds of projects, naw'mean?

Did you know your boy is a *slammin'* cook? *Flav's Fried Chicken* ("FFC") is coming to a restaurant near you. I launched the first tastings of FFC wings at my boy, Peter Cimino's, joint, *Mama Cimino's* in Las Vegas. In January 2011, we opened our first FFC restaurant in Clinton, Iowa and we got plans to go nation-wide. You tell the Colonel, I said, "Watch your back, Gee."

If you're gonna eat, you need a little something to wash it down, right? Me and my good buddy, Tony "Sex" Capamacchio, who owns a vodka company called Sex Vodka, put our heads together and came up with Le Flav Spirits. We're producing a cherry vodka, a berry vodka, an olive vodka, a sweet tea vodka, a grape vodka and a bubble gum vodka. Hey, they didn't call me "Ricco Ric, the Flavor Freak!" for nothing!

Hee, hee, har, har!

Le Flav will have a cognac, too, as well as a champagne—Chateau Le Flav. We'll even have a non-alcoholic Chateau La Flav at some point. That will be a big hit in the Muslim community, I know it.

But wait! There's more!

I met a guy named Dave Harmon, who owns an orchard in Napa Valley, and we're going to put out high end Cabernet. The bottle is etched with the image of Flavor Flav on the front and the back panel, and includes the lyrics to my songs. It's something new, and something that no other rap artist has ever done.

Why not?

I'm trying to "get in where I fit in"—and get the money, Gee.

There's still music to be made, too. I'm working on a new album, and putting together some really cool stuff that I hope you'll be listening to on your IPod pretty soon.

Public Enemy is still going strong in its 25th year, folks. You know what that means, don't you? Someone just got eligible for the Rock and Roll Hall of Fame!

The big deal is, I'm moving now in new circles, with new friends who bring positive things to my life. I'm done with the drug life and instead, my circle is full of people who are really there for me, man. You are who you associate with, and God is helping me to filter out all the negative influences that used to rule my life.

I have to be thankful for that.

Conclusion

"**F**LAV, YOU REALLY OUGHT TO WRITE A BOOK."

People been saying that to me for years, and I always thought I would do it someday, but I never felt like the time was right. After all, I'm not finished yet. I've always thought that the best was still ahead for me. Why write a book now, when it's gonna leave out the best part?

Hee, hee, har, har!

I still feel that way, but I guess as I get older, I get more appreciation for the journey I've already taken, naw'mean? I understand that life isn't promised—hell, *tomorrow* isn't promised. The only sure thing about this life is death. And that's the truth.

So I figure, now is the time.

Now is the time because I have already been through some serious shit, naw'mean? I started life as William

Jonathan Drayton, but created myself as "Flavor Flav." I started with music—and music has never left me and never will—but I also created myself as a television personality. I started as a thrill seeker—and lived to write a book and tell you all about it! Hee, hee, har, har!

I climbed to the deep hole of drug addiction and touched the bottom, then climbed out of it, a different person, man. I climbed out and you know what was waiting for your boy? Love, a home (a couple of them, actually) and good friends—things I can appreciate now because I know what it's like to be without them.

So that's it. That's my story—or all of it that's written, right now.

For the rest, folks, you'll just have to wait.

I'm not finished yet.

Shout Outs

I MET A GUY who became my good friend, Rick Willard. He created the ATM card and the first pre-paid phone card ever. He also happens to be one of my best friends in Vegas. He loves cigars. His cigar room is the size of a hotel suite!

Then there's Edward Mumford, who says that he got me into the American Music Awards once. I didn't remember him when he first re-introduced himself, but now, he and his son, Chad, are some of my best friends.

There's Tom Karras and his cousin George who run a place called "Screwballs" that's my favorite place to go when I'm in Las Vegas.

My cousin Greg—Clifton G. Johnson—who stepped in and became my manager around the time I had that big problem with Def Jam and the solo album project. He's worked side by side with me for the past 14 years and now manages

Public Enemy, too. Greg used to be the CFO for GAP, Banana Republic and Old Navy. He went to school at North Carolina A & T and I remember when *PE* used to go to North Carolina to perform—long before he became my manager—he would always come to my shows. He was the only family member who would come out like that, every time, no matter what. Through Greg, I was able to be a guest drum major for the North Carolina A&T marching band with my boy Dr. Rough, my boy, Stuff and my boy, Aaron. Greg looks out for your boy—and I'm grateful to him.

Shout outs to my god-children: Latasha Rose Leonard, Tia Nicole Allen, Deja Monet Eason, Brandon Bazil, Rashad Dante Walker, Keisha Brooks, Lameke Black, Sofia Palermo Chavez, Tayvon Arroyo, Elijah Jamie.

There are so many others—family, friends, and fans. I'm gonna run down all their names, right here. Hey yo! I named you in my book:

Andy Heyward; Antonio Fargas; LeVert; Charlie Wilson; George and Gavin Maloof; Marilyn Manson; Gus from Gus Fashions in St. Louis; Payback; Bistroll at Do It Fluid; the rapper DMX; Lyor Cohen; Hydro; Dave Pagan from Southpoint Casino; Betsy Hammer; Rodney Allen Rippy; Sir Jinx; Ken; Jim Brown; Andrew Courtney and Greg at Hard Rock Café on the Vegas Strip; Evelyn and Courtney at Mandalay Bay Hotel and Casino; my boys from the block in the Bronx: Eric Phazo, Lex, RaRa, Big John; Indji Bessim, Esq. and

Elizabeth Zagajeski, Esq.; Brigitte; the rapper YoYo; DJ Quick; Sammy Kim; Yasu; Eric Ortner and Ron Popeil.

Let me not forget Al & Penny Guthry, Tasha Smith, and Jimmy "Jay" Smith.

My shout out to Chriss Angel...

Yo, Chriss, you are the best magician alive and that ever lived in this lifetime...You are the real deal, my man. Every time you do your magic, it always blows me away. Even if I seen the trick before, it's always like my first time seeing it every time. Keep doin' like you do, Chriss, and most of all thanks for being a friend to your boy Flavor Flav.

Rest in peace Bernie Mac...

Can't forget you Steve Harvey...

Last but not least.....Norris and Sir Jinx.

I've also got to thank the people who made this book possible: Dr. Farrah Gray, Karyn Folan, Dr. Marcia Brevard Wynn and all the people at Farrah Gray Publishing. Thank you!

If I left you out, I'm sorry. I didn't mean to. So many people have helped me in my life, and still do, that all I can say is, I love you and I'll get you on the next one!

Flavor Flav's Famous Pepper Steak

1 ¼ lbs boneless round steak, ½ inch thick cut into thin strips
1 medium green pepper, julienned
1 medium onion, julienned
2 tablespoons butter
2 (15 ounce) cans tomato sauce
1 (8 ounce) package fresh mushrooms, sliced
1½ teaspoons salt
1 teaspoon dried basil
¼ teaspoon pepper
1 (16 ounce) package fettuccine
⅓ cup shredded parmesan cheese

In a large skillet, sauté the steak, green pepper and onion in butter until the meat is no longer pink. Stir in tomato sauce, mushrooms, salt, basil and pepper. Bring to a boil. Reduce heat, cover and simmer for 20–25 minutes or until meat is tender. Cook fettuccine according to package directions, drain. Top with steak mixture and sprinkle with parmesan cheese.

Flavor Flav's Famous Cheddar and Penne

2 tablespoons and 1½ teaspoons olive oil
2½ pounds sweet Italian pork sausage, cut into ½-inch slices
2½ large green pepper, cut into 2-inch-long strips
2½ large onion, sliced
7½ cloves garlic, minced
2½ (10.75 ounce) cans Campbell's® Condensed Cheddar Cheese Soup
1¼ cups milk
5 cups penne pasta, cooked and drained

Heat the oil in a 10-inch skillet over medium-high heat. Add the sausage and cook until well browned, stirring occasionally. Remove the sausage from the skillet. Pour off any fat.

Add the pepper and onion to the skillet and cook until the vegetables are tender, stirring occasionally. Add the garlic and cook and stir for 1 minute. Stir in the soup and milk and heat to a boil. Return the sausage to the skillet. Reduce the heat to low. Cook until the sausage is cooked through, stirring occasionally.

Place the pasta into a large bowl. Add the sausage mixture and toss to coat.

Flavor Flav's Famous Chicken Cacciatore

2 cups all-purpose flour for coating
½ teaspoon salt
1/4 teaspoon ground black pepper
1 (4 pound) chicken, cut into pieces
2 tablespoons vegetable oil
1 onion, chopped
2 cloves garlic, minced
1 green bell pepper, chopped
1 (14.5 ounce) can diced tomatoes
½ teaspoon dried oregano
½ cup white wine
2 cups fresh mushrooms, quartered
salt and pepper to taste

Combine the flour, salt and pepper in a plastic bag. Shake the chicken pieces in flour until coated. Heat the oil in a large skillet *(one that has a cover/lid)*. Fry the chicken pieces until they are browned on both sides. Remove from skillet.

Add the onion, garlic and bell pepper to the skillet and sauté until the onion is slightly browned. Return the chicken to the skillet and add the tomatoes, oregano and wine. Cover and simmer for 30 minutes over medium low heat.

Add the mushrooms and salt and pepper to taste. Simmer for 10 more minutes.

Flavor Flav's Famous Mamma Mia Sauce

¾ cup chopped onion

5 cloves garlic, minced

¼ cup olive oil

2 (28 ounce) cans whole peeled tomatoes

2 teaspoons salt

1 teaspoon white sugar

1 bay leaf

1 (6 ounce) can tomato paste

¾ teaspoon dried basil

½ teaspoon ground black pepper

In a large saucepan over medium heat, sauté onion and garlic in olive oil until onion is translucent. Stir in tomatoes, salt, sugar and bay leaf. Cover, reduce heat to low, and simmer 90 minutes. Stir in tomato paste, basil, ½ teaspoon pepper simmer for 30 more minutes.

Son of Legendary King of Reggae Music Bob Marley

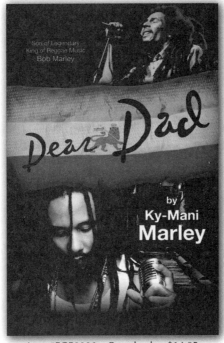

Item #FGP9996 • Paperback • $14.95

Ky-Mani Marley's memoir, *Dear Dad*, is a compelling biographical exegesis of a son who was locked out of his iconic father's shelter for the first half of his life and forced to survive the bleak poverty and bloodied predatory environment of Miami's most violent ghetto streets. This compellingly told narrative chronicles young Ky-Mani's gritty ascent from a bullet-riddled life to the world stages he now commands as a Grammy nominated and Billboard #1 chart-topping musical artist.

Learn the Nine Key Principles to Success

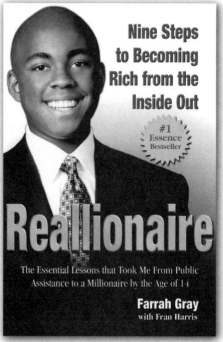

Nine Steps to Becoming Rich from the Inside Out

#1 Essence Bestseller

Realionaire

The Essential Lessons that Took Me From Public Assistance to a Millionaire by the Age of 14

Farrah Gray
with Fran Harris

Code 2246 • Paperback • $14.95

A remarkable teenager who went from public assistance to a million dollar net worth, Farrah Gray shares the principles of success he learned along the way. His story is a step-by-step primer for others to create success in their own lives with honor, charity, and compassion.